John Blatchford, Charles Ira Bushnell

The Narrative of John Blatchford

Detailing His Sufferings in the Revolutionary War

John Blatchford, Charles Ira Bushnell

The Narrative of John Blatchford
Detailing His Sufferings in the Revolutionary War

ISBN/EAN: 9783744761505

Printed in Europe, USA, Canada, Australia, Japan

Cover: Foto ©ninafisch / pixelio.de

More available books at **www.hansebooks.com**

THE
NARRATIVE
OF
JOHN BLATCHFORD,

DETAILING

His sufferings in the Revolutionary War, while a Prisoner with the British.

AS RELATED BY HIMSELF.

WITH

AN INTRODUCTION AND NOTES,

BY

CHARLES I. BUSHNELL.

NEW YORK:
PRIVATELY PRINTED.
1865.

Entered, according to Act of Congress, in the year 1865, by

CHARLES I. BUSHNELL,

In the Clerk's Office of the District Court of the United States for the Southern District of New York.

TO

CAPT. JOHN BLATCHFORD,

OF ROCKPORT, MASS.,

ELDEST SURVIVING SON OF THE

HERO OF THIS NARRATIVE,

THIS TRACT

IS RESPECTFULLY

DEDICATED.

INTRODUCTION.

JOHN BLATCHFORD, the hero of this narrative, was the son of John Blatchford, of Sandy Bay, now Rockport, on Cape Ann, in the commonwealth of Massachusetts, and was born about the year 1762.

After receiving a very limited education, he was brought up to the occupation of a fisherman, which employment he pursued until the month of June, 1777, when, being about fifteen years of age, he enlisted as a cabin-boy on board the Hancock, a continental ship, commanded by Capt. John Manly.

On the 8th day of July following, the Hancock was captured by the British ship Rainbow, Sir George Collier, and her crew taken to Halifax and imprisoned. After being immured there awhile, and treated with great severity, our hero was sent to England, and soon after his arrival there was put on board an Indiaman, and transported with eighty-two other Americans to the East Indies, where he was compelled first to do duty as a soldier, and then to work in the pepper gardens belonging to the East India Company. He eventually, with great risk and after great suffering, effected his escape, and ultimately reached Guadaloupe, one of the West India Islands, where he took passage for Philadelphia; but misfortune again befell him, for while on his way thither, he was captured by the enemy, taken to New York, and put on board the prison ship "Jersey." After remaining in this wretched hulk about a week, he was sent in a cartel to France, whence in course of time he returned home, after an absence of almost six years, having, during his long imprisonment, endured the severest hardships and privations, experienced the most barbarous treatment from the hands of the British, and made several narrow escapes from death, not only from the bayonet, but from hunger and disease, and likewise from the attack of savage beasts of prey.

Soon after his return, he married Anna, the daughter of Nehemiah Grover, a farmer by occupation, and a respectable landholder. Mr. Blatchford resumed the avocation of a fisherman, which he followed for a short time, and then took to the seas for a livelihood, making many voyages to foreign countries. He died at Port au Prince, in the West Indies, about the year 1794, and was buried in that town. He left surviving him his widow, and also two sons and one daughter, to mourn their untimely loss.

In his stature, our hero was about medium height. He had broad shoulders, full chest, and well-proportioned limbs. His complexion was sallow, his eyes dark, and his hair black and curly. He was temperate in his habits, dignified in his deportment, and though possessed of great muscular power and most undaunted courage, he was, nevertheless, peaceful in his disposition and slow to anger.

The narrative of his adventures while a prisoner, was undoubtedly prepared from dictation. It is an interesting, romantic, and in many respects, an extraordinary document. It is remarkable for the series of misfortunes which befell its hero, and as a record of malignant spite and savage brutality on the part of the British, is almost unparalleled in the annals of history.

It was originally published in New London in 1788, and was issued in pamphlet form. In the year 1797, a lengthy abstract appeared in the columns of Freneau's "Time Piece," a paper published in the city of New York. In July, 1860, the entire production was printed in the "Cape Ann

Gazette," and the demand for copies having far exceeded the edition, it was reproduced in the same paper in the month of October following. We will further state that the present edition has been printed from a certified copy, which through the courtesy of the Massachusetts Historical Society, we were permitted to have made from one of the original tracts now in its possession.

THE "JERSEY" PRISON SHIP.

NARRATIVE

OF

Remarkable Occurrences,

IN THE LIFE OF

JOHN BLATCHFORD,

Of *Cape-Ann*, Commonwealth of *Massachusetts*,

CONTAINING,

His treatment in *Nova-Scotia*—the *West Indies*—*Great-Britain*—*France*, and the *East-Indies*, as a prisoner in the late war.

Taken from his own mouth.

NEW LONDON: Printed by T. GREEN.

M,DCC,LXXX,VIII.

[With the privilege of Copy-Right]

NARRATIVE.

IN June, 1777, I shipped myself as cabin-boy on board the Continental ship Hancock, (1) John Manly, Esq. (2) commander, being then in the 15th year of my age, and a few days after sailed on a cruize. Being out some days we fell in with and took the Fox, (3) a British frigate of 28 guns, after an engagement of four glasses. Our captain sent on board the prize as many men as we could spare, and both ships kept company several days, till on the 8th of July we fell in with the British ships Rainbow (4) of 40 guns, and Flora (5) of 32 guns (who had in company the brig Cabot (₆) of 16 guns which had just before been taken by the Milford British frigate) (₇) by whom we were both taken (₈) and carried into Halifax.

I was kept prisoner among a number of my countrymen, on board the Rainbow, until we arrived at Halifax. (₉) On our arrival there we were taken on shore and confined in a prison which had formerly been a sugar house. (₁₀)—The large number of prisoners confined in this house (near 300) together with a scanty allowance of provisions, occasioned it to be very sickly. So irksome a situation put us upon meditating an escape—but we could form no plan that was likely to be attended with success, till George Barnard, who had been a midshipman in the Hancock, and who was confined in the same room with myself, concerted a plan to release us, which was to be effected by diging a small passage under ground, to extend to a garden that was behind the prison and without the prison wall, where we might make a breach in the night with safety, and probably all obtain our liberty.— This plan greatly elated our spirits, and we were all anxious to proceed immediately in executing of it.

Our cabins were built one above another, from the floor to the height of a man's head ; and mine being one of those built on the floor, was pitched upon to be taken up:—this being done, six of us agreed to do the work, whose names were, George Barnard and William Atkins of Boston, (late midshipmen in the Hancock), Lemuel Fowle of Cape-Ann, Isaiah Churchill of Plimouth, Asa Cole of Weathersfield, and myself. We took up the cabin and cut a hole in the plank underneath.

The sugar-house stood upon a foundation of stone which raised the floor four feet above the ground, and gave us sufficient room to work and to convey away the dirt that we dug up.

The instruments which we had to work with were one scraper, one long spike, and some sharp sticks; with these we proceeded in our difficult undertaking. As the hole was too small to admit of more than one person to work at a time, we dug by turns ten or twelve days, and carried the dirt in our bosoms to another end of the cellar; by this time we supposed we had dug far enough, and word was given out among the prisoners to prepare themselves for flight. But while we were in the midst of gaiety, congratulating each other upon our happy prospects, we were basely betrayed by one of our own countrymen whose name was Knowles: he had been a midshipman on board the Boston frigate, (n) and was put on board the Fox when she was taken by the Hancock and Boston.—What could have induced him to commit so vile an action cannot be conceived, as no advantage could accrue to him from our detection, and death was the certain consequence to many of his miserable countrymen—that it was so, is all I can say. A few hours before we were to have attempted our escape, Knowles informed the sergeant of the guard (Mr. Bible) of our design; and by his treachery lost his country the lives of more than a hundred valuable citizens—fathers and husbands—whose return would have rejoiced the hearts of now weeping fatherless children, and called forth tears of joy from wives, now helpless and disconsolate widows—When we were discovered, the whole guard was ordered into the room; and being informed by Knowles who it was that performed the work, we were all six confined in irons—the hole was filled up, and a centinel constantly placed in the room, to prevent any further attempt.—We were all kept in close confinement till two of my fellow-sufferers Barnard and Cole, died; one of which was put into the ground with his irons on his hands. (12) I was afterwards permitted to walk the yard. But as my irons were too small and caused my hands to swell, and made them very sore, I asked the sergeant to take them off and give me larger ones,—he being a person of humanity, and compassionating my sufferings, changed my irons for others that were larger, and more easy to my hands.

Knowles, who was likewise permitted to walk the yard, for his perfidy, would take every opportunity to insult and mortify me, by asking me whether I wanted to run away again? and when I was going home, &c?—His daily affronts, together with his conduct in betraying of his countrymen, so exasperated me, that I wished for nothing more than for an opportunity to convince him that I did not love him.—One day as he was tantalizing over me as usual, I suddenly drew one hand out of my irons, flew at him and struck him in the face, knocked out two or three of his teeth, and bruised his mouth very much. He cried out, that the prisoner had got loose,—but before any assistance came, I had put my hand again into the hand-cuff, and was walking about the yard as usual. When the guard came, they demanded of me in what manner I struck him? I told them with both my hands.

They then tried to pull my hands out, but could not, and concluded it must be as I had said;—some laughed and some were angry—but in the end I was ordered again into prison. The next day I was sent on board the Greyhound frigate, (¹²) capt. Dickson, (¹³) bound on a cruize in Boston-bay. After being out a few days, we met with a severe gale of wind, in which we sprung our main-mast and received considerable other damage. We were then obliged to bear away for the West-Indies, and on our passage fell in with and took a brig from Norwich, laden with stock, &c. The captain and hands were put on board a Danish vessel the same day. We carried the brig into Antigua,* where we immediately repaired, and were ordered in company with the Vulture sloop of war (¹⁴) to convoy a fleet of merchantmen to New-York. We left the fleet off Sandy-Hook, and sailed for Philadelphia, where

* One of the West India islands, Leeward Group.

we lay till we were made a packet and ordered for Halifax with dispatches. We had a quick passage, and arrived safe. While we lay in the road, admiral Byron (16) arrived* in the Princess Royal (17) from England, who being short of men, and we having a surplusage for a packet, many of our men were ordered on board the Princess-Royal, and among them most of our boat's crew.

Soon after, some of the officers going on shore, I was ordered into the boat.—We landed at the Governor's-slip—it being then near night. This was the first time since I had been on board the Greyhound that I had had an opportunity to escape from her, as they were before this particularly careful of me; therefore I was determined to get away then if possible, and to effect it I waded round a wharf and went up a by-way, (fearing I should meet the officers): I soon got into the street and made the best of my way towards Irishtown,† where I expected to be safe;—but unfortunately while running, I was met and stopped by an emissary,

---

* Admiral Byron arrived at Halifax, August 26, 1778.
† The southern suburbs of Halifax, chiefly inhabited by the Irish population.

who demanded of me my business, and where I was going? I endeavoured to deceive him, that he might let me pass; but it was in vain—he ordered me to follow him:—

I offered him what money I had (about $\frac{7}{6}$ sterl.) to let me go—this too was ineffectual. I then told him I was an American and making my escape from a long confinement, and was determin'd to pass, and took up a stone. He immediately drew his bayonet* and ordered me to go back with him.—I refused, and told him to keep his distance.—He then run upon me, and pushing his bayonet into my side, it came out near my navel; but the wound was not very deep;—he then made a second pass, and stabbed me through my arm: he was about to stab me a third time, when I struck him with the stone and knocked him down. I then run, but the guard which had been alarmed, immediately took me, and carried me before the governor (Hughes) (i.) where I understood the man was dead. I was

* Bayonets were invented at Bayonne, in France, 1670, and received their name from the town where they were invented. They were first used by the English, Sept. 24, 1693, and superseded the pike completely under William III.

threatened with every kind of death, and ordered out of the governor's presence.

Whilst in confinement I was informed by a young gentleman (who was to be sent to England and tried for killing a man in a duel) that it was not in the power of the Governor to try me; but that I should be sent to England; which I found to be true. The next day I was sent on board the Greyhound, the ship I had run from, and we sailed for England. Our captain being a humane man, ordered my irons off, a few days after we sailed, and permitted me to do duty as formerly. Being out thirteen days we spoke the Hazard (19) sloop of war, who inform'd that the French fleet was then cruising in the English channel: (20)—for this reason we put into Cork, and the dispatches were forwarded to England.—While we lay in the Cove of Cork,* I jumped overboard, with intention of getting away; but unfortunately I was discovered and fired at by the marines: the boat was immediately sent after

* A seaport town in Ireland, now called Queenstown—so named by the sycophantic inhabitants of the place, in honor of the Queen's visit there in 1849. The old classic name was infinitely preferable.

me, took me up and carried me on board again. At this time almost all the officers were on shore, and the ship was left in charge of the sailing-master, one Drummond, who beat me most cruelly;—to get out of his way I run forward—he followed me, and as I was running back he came up with me and threw me down the mainhold.* The fall, together with the beating, was so severe that I was deprived of my senses for a considerable time; when I recovered them I found myself in the carpenter's birth, placed upon some old canvass, between two chests, having my right thigh, leg and arm broken, and several parts of my body severely bruised. In this situation I lay eighteen days, till our officers, (who had been on business to Dublin) came on board. The captain enquired for the prisoner, and being informed of my situation, came down with the doctor to set my bones, but finding them callussed they concluded not to meddle with me.

The ship lay at Cork till the French fleet left the

* That part of a ship just before the main mast, and which generally contained the fresh water and beer for the use of the ship's company.

channel, and then sailed for Spithead.*—On our arrival there I was sent in irons on board the Princess-Amelia, (21) and the next day was carried on board the Britannia (22) in Portsmouth † harbour, to be tried before Sir Thomas Pye, (23) lord high admiral of England, and president of the court-martial.

Before the officers had collected, I was put under the care of a centinel; and the seamen and women who came on board compassionated my sufferings, which rather heightened than diminished my distress. I was sitting under the awning, almost overpowered by the reflection of my unhappy situation, every moment expecting to be summoned for my trial, when I heard somebody enquiring for the prisoner—supposing it to be an officer, I rose up and answered, that I was there. The gentleman came to me, told me to be of good chear, and taking out a bottle of cordial bid me drink, which I did:—

* A celebrated roadstead off the southern coast of England, one of the principal rendezvous of the British navy, so secure from all winds except the S. E., as to have been termed by sailors "the king's bed-chamber."

† A fortified seaport town, and the principal naval station of England.

he then enquired where I belonged—I informed him—he asked me if I had parents living, and if I had any friends in England?—I answered I had neither: he then assured me he was my friend, and would render me all the assistance in his power.—He then enquired of me every circumstance relative to my fray with the man at Halifax, for whose death I was now to be tried;—and instructed me what to say on my trial,—told me if it was asked in court " if I had any friend or attorney to speak for me," to look at such a corner of the state-room, where I should see him, and to answer the court " Yes, Mr. Thomas," for that was the gentleman's name. All this was spoken in so friendly a manner, that I could not distrust him, although what he had instructed me to say, appeared to me, would be against myself.

The court having assembled, I was called in and examined partly, and on being asked " If I had any friend to speak in my behalf," I looked round, and saw Mr. Thomas, and answered, " Yes, Mr. Thomas," who then came forward.—The court asked him what he had to say in behalf of the prisoner?—On which he desired them to question the prisoner, and if he could not answer sufficiently, he would speak for him. I was then asked if I meant to kill the man. I answered as instructed (tho' loth) that I did. The court seemed surpriz'd and asked me the question again, and I again answered, Yes. I was then asked if I should have hurt the man had he not molested me? I replied, No.—I was then asked many other questions, and if I was not sorry I had undertaken in the rebellion against my king?—Mr. Thomas then spoke, and said it was hardly fair to ask me such a question upon this occasion; and that considering my youth, I had given as fair an account of myself as could be expected.—He spoke a considerable time on the subject, and concluded with comparing our combat to a field battle between two armies—expatiated largely and explained the subject so clearly that no answer was made to his arguments.—I was ordered to withdraw, and waited with painful impatience to know my destiny.—This was repeated two or three times, till at last I was called in and acquitted of the murder, and was informed that I was to be sent back to Halifax, to be exchanged as a prisoner of war. I cannot express my feelings on this occasion, and no one can know them, but by experiencing the same reverse of fortune.

I immediately found my benefactor and returned him thanks, with gratitude for his friendly and benevolent assistance. Mr. Thomas then asked the liberty of taking me on shore with him, engaging to return me the next day—and liberty was granted him.—He told a young lad, his son, to walk with me about Portsmouth, and shew me the town, and then to carry me home to his house; which he did. In the evening Mr. Thomas came into the kitchen and asked me to walk into the parlour, to satisfy the curiosity of some ladies, who had never seen a Yankee, as they called me: I went in, and they seemed greatly surprized to see me look like an Englishman; they said they were sure I was no Yankee, but like themselves. The idea they had formed of the Americans was nearly the same as we have of the natives of this country. When the ladies had satisfied their curiosity, Mr. Thomas put a guinea into his hat, and carrying it round asked the ladies to contribute for the poor Yankee: he then gave me the money, (about four guineas.)

The next morning I was sent on board the Princess-Amelia, where I spent a joyful day; expecting soon to be sent on board the Greyhound, which was bound to Halifax.

In the evening I heard a boat coming along-side, and supposing it to belong to the Greyhound, (as the people in the boat enquired for me)—I made haste and jumped into the boat; but to my extreme disappointment and grief, I was carried on board an Indiaman, and immediately put down into the run,* where I was confined seven days. I begged that I might send word on shore to my former benefactor, and inform him of my situation, but they would not grant it. On the seventh day, I heard the boatswain pipe all hands, and about noon I was called up on deck, when I found myself on board the Princess-Royal (24) indiaman, captain Robert Kerr;—we were then off the Isle of Wight, bound to the East-Indies, in company with six others, viz. the Ceres, Hawke, Prince, Sandwich, Walpole and True-Briton, all

* The run of a ship is that part of her hull under water which comes narrower by degrees from the floor timbers to the sternposts.

large ships, (25) belonging to the East-India company. (26).

Our captain told me, if I behaved well and did my duty, I should receive as good usage as any man on board :—this gave me great encouragement. I now found my destiny was fixed—that whatever I could do, would not in the least alter my situation, and therefore was determined to do the best I could, and make myself as contented as my unfortunate situation would admit.

After being on board several days, I found there were in the Princess-Royal, eighty-two Americans, all destined to the East-Indies, for being what they called Rebels. (27)

We had a passage of seventeen weeks to St. Helena, where we put in and landed part of our cargo, (which consisted wholly of provisions), and some of the soldiers who were brought out for that island. The ship lay here about three weeks; we then sailed for Batavia*—and on the passage touched at the Cape of Good-Hope,† where we

---

* Capital and seaport town of the island of Java.

† The Cape of Good Hope was first discovered by Bartholomew Diaz, 1486—first doubled by Vasco de Gama, 1497—

found the whole of the fleet that sailed with us from England—we took in some provisions and necessaries and set sail for Batavia, where we arrived in ten weeks. Here we purchased a large quantity of arrack and remained a considerable time.

We then sailed for Bencoolen,* in the island of Sumatria, and after a passage of about six weeks arrived there, (this was in June 1780). At this place the Americans were all carried on shore; and I found that I was no longer to remain on board the ship, but condemned to serve as a soldier for five years.—I offered to bind myself to the captain for five years, or any longer term, if I might serve on board the ship:—he told me it was impossible for me to be released from acting as a soldier, unless I could pay fifty pounds sterling. As I was unable to do this, I was obliged to go through the manual exercise with the other prisoners; among whom was William Randall of Boston, and Josiah Folgier of Nantucket, both young men, and one of them an

---

planted by Holland, 1651—taken by the British, 1795—again in 1806, and definitely ceded to Great Britain, 1814.

‡ Bencouloo, corruptly called Bencoolen, is on the S. W. coast of the island of Sumatra. The chief trade is pepper.

old ship-mate of mine;—these two and myself agreed to behave as ignorant and aukward as possible; and what motions we learned one day we were to forget the next.—We pursued this conduct near a fortnight, and were beaten every day by the drill-sergeant, who exercised us; and when he found we were determined in our obstinacy, and that it was not possible for him to learn us anything, we were all three sent into the pepper gardens belonging to the East-India company, and continued picking peppers from morning till night, and allowed but two scanty meals a day;—this, together with the amazing heat of the sun, (the island lying under the equator) was too much for an American constitution, unused to a hot climate, and we expected that we should soon end our misery and our lives;—but Providence still preserved us for greater hardships.*

* Sumatria is an island of the Indian ocean, situated between 93 and 104 degrees of East longitude, and between 5 degrees and 30 minutes North and 5 degrees and 30 minutes South latitude; extending from N. W. to S. E. 900 miles long, and from 100 to 150 broad, separated from the continent of the Further India by the straits of Malacca on the N. E. and from the island of Java by the straits of Sunda on the S. E. This

The Americans died daily with heat and hard fare, which determined my two companions and myself in an endeavour to make our escape.—We had been in the pepper gardens four months when an opportunity offered, and we resolved upon trying our fortune;—Folgier, Randall and myself sat out with an intention of reaching Croy, (a small harbour where the Dutch often touch at to water) on the opposite side of the island.—Folgier had by some means got a bayonet, which he fixed on the end of a stick—Randall and myself had nothing but staves, which were all the weapons we carried with us. We provided ourselves with fire-works* for our journey, which we pursued unmolested till the fourth day just at night, when we heard a rustling in the bushes and discovered nine seapoys, (country-born soldiers in the British service) who suddenly rushed out upon us.

Folgier being the most resolute of us, run at one

island lying under the equator, and the low grounds near the sea-coast being flooded one-half of the year, is very unhealthful. The natives build most of their houses upon pillars, to secure them against the annual inundations.
(This note was in the original edition.—Ed.)

* Tinder box and accompaniments for striking fire.

of them and pushed his bayonet through his body
into a tree; Randall knocked down another;—but
they overpowered us, bound us, and carried us back
to the fort, which we reached in one day and half,
though we had been four days travelling from it,
owing to the circle we made by going round the
shore; and they came across the woods, being
acquainted with the way. Immediately on our
arrival at the fort the governor* called a court-
martial, to have us tried.—We were soon all condemned to be shot the next morning at seven
o'clock, and ordered to be sent into the dungeon
and confined in irons, where we were attended by
an adjutant who brought a priest with him to pray
and converse with us;—but Folgier, who hated the
name and sight of an Englishman, desired that we
might be left alone, and not be troubled with any
company:—the clergyman reprimanded him, and
told him he made very light of his situation, on
supposition that he would be reprieved; but if he
expected it he deceived himself:—Folgier still per-
sisted in the clergyman's leaving of us, if he would

* The governor of Fort Marlborough at this time was
William Broff, Esq. He held the position from 1772 to 1783.

have us make our peace with God ; for, said he, the sight of Englishmen, from whom we have received such treatment, is more disagreeable than the evil spirits of whom you have spoken :—that if he could have his choice, he would choose death in preference to life, if he must have it on conditions of such barbarous usage as he had received from their hands ; and that the thoughts of death did not seem so hideous to him as his past sufferings. He visited us again about midnight, but finding his company was not acceptable, he soon left us to our own melancholy reflections.

Before sun-rise we heard the drums beat, and soon after heard the direful noise of the door grating on its iron hinges—we were all taken out, our irons taken off, and we conducted by a strong guard of soldiers to the parade, surrounded by a circle of armed men, and led into the midst of them, where three white coffins were placed by our side :—silence was then commanded, and the adjutant taking a paper out of his pocket read our sentence :—and now I cannot describe my feelings upon this occasion, nor can it be felt by any one but those who have experienced some remarkable deliverance from the grim hand of death, when surrounded on all sides, and nothing but death expected from every quarter, and by Divine Providence there is some way found out for escape—so it seemed to me when the adjutant pulled out another paper from his pocket and read, "that the governor and council, in consideration of the youth of Randall and myself, (supposing us to be led on by Folgier, who was the eldest) thought fit to pardon us from death, and that instead we were to receive eight hundred lashes each;"—although this last sentence appeared terrible to me, yet in comparison with death, it seemed to be light.—Poor Folgier was shot in our presence—previous to which we were told we might go and converse with him—Randall went and talked with him first, and after him I went up to take my leave, but my feelings were such at the time that I had not power to utter a single word to my departing friend, who seemed as undaunted and seemingly as willing to die as I was willing to be released—and told me not to forget the promises we had formerly made each other, which was, to embrace the first opportunity to escape:—we parted, and he was immediately after shot dead. We were next taken and tied ; and the adjutant brought a small whip made of cotton, which consisted of a number of strands and knotted at the ends ; but these knots were all cut off by the adjutant before the drummer took it, which made it not worse than to have been whipt with cotton yarn. After being whipped 800 lashes we were sent to the company hospital, where we had been about three weeks, when Randall told me he intended very soon to make his escape :— this somewhat surprized me, as I had lost all hopes of regaining my liberty, and supposed he had :—I told him I had hoped he would never mention it again ; but however, if that was his design I would accompany him. He advised me, (if I was fearful) to tarry behind ;—but finding he was determined on going, I resolved to run the risque once more ; and as we were then in the hospital we were not suspected of such a design.

Having provided ourselves with fire-works and knives, about the first of December 1780, we sat out, with intention of reaching the Dutch settlement of Croy, which is but about two or three hundred miles distance upon a direct line, but as we were obliged to travel along the sea coast, (fearing to risque the nearest way) it was a journey of eight hundred miles. We took each a stick and hung round our neck, and every day cut a notch, which was the method we took to keep time.—In this manner we travelled, living on fruit, turtle-eggs and some turtle, which we cooked every night with the fire we built to sleep by to secure us from wild beasts—they being here in great plenty, such as buffaloes, tigers, jackanapes, leopards, lions, baboons and monkies. On the 30th day of our travelling we met with nothing we could eat, and found no water—at night we found some fruit which appeared to the eye to be very delicious, (different from any we had seen in our travel) it resembled a fruit which grows in the West-Indies, called a Jack, (?) about the size of an orange:—we being very dry and hungry immediately gathered some of this fruit—but finding it of a sweet sickish taste I eat but two--Randall eat freely:—in the evening we found we were poisoned: I was sick and puked considerably:—Randall was sick and began to swell all round his body; he grew worse all night, but continued to have his senses till the next day, when he died, and left me to mourn my greater wretched-

ness,—more than 400 miles from any settlement—
no companion—the wide ocean on one side and a
prowling wilderness on the other—liable to many
kinds of deaths, more terrible than being shot. I
laid down by Randall's body, wishing if possible
that he might return and tell me what course to
take.—My thoughts almost distracted me, so that I
was unable to do anything till the next day; during
all which time I continued by the side of Randall—
I then got up and made a hole in the sand and
buried him.

I now continued my journey as well as my weak
state of body would permit;—the weather being at
this time extreme hot and rainy.—I frequently lay
down and would wish that I might never rise
again :—despair had almost wholly possessed me;
and sometimes in a kind of delirium would fancy I
heard my mother's voice, and my friends calling
me, and I would answer them :—at other times my
wild imagination would paint to my view scenes
which I was well acquainted with, then supposing
myself near home I would run as fast as my
feeble legs could carry me :—frequently I fancied
that I heard dogs bark, men cutting wood, and

every noise which I have heard in my native country.

One day as I was travelling, a small dog, as I thought it to be, came fawning round me and followed me, but I soon discovered it to be a young lion;—I supposed that its dam must be nigh, and therefore run; it followed me sometime and then left me; I proceeded on, but had not got far from it before it began to cry; I looked round and saw a lioness making towards it—she yelled most frightfully, which greatly terrified me; but she laid down something from her mouth for her young one, and then with another yell turned and went off from me.

Some days after, I was travelling by the edge of a woods, (which from its appearance had felt severely the effects of a tornado or hurricane, the trees being all torn up by the roots) and I heard a cracking noise in the bushes—looking about I saw a monstrous large tiger making slowly towards me, which frightened me exceedingly; when he had approached within a few rods of me, in my surprize I suddenly lifted up my hands and hollowed very loud: this sudden noise frightened him, seemingly as much as I had been, and he immediately turned and run into the woods, and I saw him no more. After this I continued travelling on without molestation, only from the monkies, who were here so plenty that oftentimes I saw them in large droves: sometimes I run from them as if afraid of them; they would then follow, grin and chatter at me, and when they got near I would turn, and they would run back into the woods, and climb the trees to get out of my way.

It was now fifteen weeks since I had left the hospital—I had travelled most all the day without any water, and began to be very thirsty, when I heard the sound of running water, as it were down a fall of rocks—I had heard it a considerable time, and at last began to suspect it was nothing but imaginary, as many other noises I had before thought to have heard. I however went on as fast as I could, and at length discovered a brook—on approaching of it I was not a little surprized and rejoiced at the sight of a Female Indian, who was fishing at the brook:—she had no other dress on than that which mother nature affords impartially to all her children, except a small cloth which she wore round her waist,—I knew not how to address myself to her:— I was afraid if I spoke she would run—and therefore I made a small noise; upon which she looked round and, seeing me, run across the brook, seemingly much frightened, leaving her fishing-line. I went up to her basket which contained five or six fish that looked much like our trout. I took up the basket and attempted to wade across where she had passed, but was too weak to wade across in that place, and went further up the stream, where I passed over—and then looking for the indian woman I saw her at some distance behind a large cocoa-nut tree:—I walked towards her, but dare not keep my eyes steadily upon her lest she should run from me as she did before.—I called to her in English; and she answered in her own tongue, which I could not understand. I then called to her in the Malays, which I understood a little of:—she answered me in a kind of surprize, and asked me in the name of *Oerum Footee* (the name of their god) from whence I came, and where I was going?—I answered her as well as I could in the Melais, that I was from Fort Marlborough,* and going to Croy—that I was

---

* A Factory which belonged to the British East India Co. on the western coast of the Island of Sumatra, 3 miles east of Bencoolen.

making my escape from the English, by whom I had been taken in war.—She told me that she had been taken by the Malays some years before—for that the two nations were always at war; and that she had been kept as a slave among them three years, and was then retaken by her countrymen. Whilst we were talking together she appeared to be very shy, and I durst not go nearer than a rod to her, lest she should run from me. She said that Croy, the place I was bound to, was about three miles distance—that if I would follow her she would conduct me to her countrymen who were but a small distance off.—I begged her to plead with her countrymen to spare my life,—she said she would, and assured me that if I behaved well I should not be hurt. She then conducted me to a small village, consisting of huts or wigwams. When we arrived at the village, the children that saw me were frightened and run away from me—and the women expressed a great deal of fear, and kept at a distance—but my guide called to them and told them not to be afraid, for that I was not come to hurt them, and then informed them from whence I came, and that I was going to Croy.

I told my guide that I was very hungry—and she sent the children for something for me to eat;—they came and brought me little round balls of boiled rice; and they not daring to come nigh, threw them to me—these I picked up and eat; afterwards a woman brought some rice and goats milk in a copper bason, and setting it on the ground, made signs for me to take it up and eat it, which I did, and then put the bason down again; they then poked away the bason with a stick, battered it with stones, and making a hole in the ground buried it. After that they conducted me to a small hut, and told me to tarry there till the morning, when they would conduct me to the harbour. I had but little sleep that night, and was up several times to look out, and saw two or three indians at a little distance from the hut, who I suppose were placed there to watch me. Early in the morning numbers came round the hut, and the female who was my guide, asked me where my country was? I could not make her understand, only that it was at a great distance. She then asked me if my countrymen eat men. I told her no—and seeing some goats, pointed at them and told her we eat such as them.—She then asked me what made me white, and if it was not the white rain that come upon us when we were small? (How they came by this notion I know not, but suppose that while she was over with the Malays she had heard something of snow from them, as they carry on some trade with the English at Fort Marlboro' and Bencoolen.) And as I wished to please and satisfy them, I told them that I supposed it was—for it was only in certain seasons of the year that it fell, and in hot weather when it did not fall the people grew darker till it returned and then the people all grew white again—this seemed to please them very much.

My protectress now brought a young man to me who, she said, was her brother, and who would shew me the way to the harbour;—she then cut a stick about eight feet long, and he took hold of one end and gave me the other—she told me that she had instructed her brother what to say at the harbour. He then led off and I followed. During our walk I put out my hand to him several times, and made signs of friendship—but he seemed to be afraid of me, and would look upwards and then fall flat on the ground and kiss it—this he repeated as often as

I made any sign or token of friendship to him.—
When we had got near the harbour he made a sign
for me to sit down upon a rock, which I did; he
then left me and went, as I supposed, to talk with
the people at the water concerning me; but I had
not sit long before I saw a vessel coming round a
point into the harbour.—They soon came on shore
in the boat.—I went down to them and made my
case known, and when the boat returned on board
they took me with them. It was a Dutch snow*
bound from China to Batavia; after they had
wooded and watered they set sail for Batavia:—
being out about three weeks we arrived there:—I
tarried on board her about three weeks longer, and
then got on board a Spanish ship which was from
Rio de la Plate bound to Spain, but by stress of
weather was forced to put into this port. After the
vessel had repaired we sailed for Spain. When we
made the Cape of Good-Hope we fell in with two
British cruizers of 20 guns each, who engaged us
and did the vessel considerable damage, but at

* A vessel with two masts resembling the main and fore-
masts of a ship, and a third small mast just abaft the mainmast,
carrying a sail similar to a ship's mizzen.

length we beat them off, and then run for the coast of Brazils, where we arrived safe and began to work at repairing our ship, but upon examination she was found to be not fit to proceed on her voyage, she was therefore condemned. I then left her and got on board a Portuguese snow, bound up to St. Helena, and we arrived safe at that place. I then went on shore and quitted her, and engaged in the garrison there to do duty as a soldier for my provisions, till some ship should arrive there bound to England. After serving here a month, I entered on board a ship called the Stormont(29)—but orders were soon after received that no indiaman should sail without convoy; and we lay here six months, during which time our captain (Montgomery) died.

While I was at St. Helena, the vessel which I came out from England in arrived here, homeward bound; she being on the return from her second voyage since I came from England:—and now I made known my case to Captain Kerr, who readily took me on board the Princess-Royal, and used me kindly—and those of my old shipmates on board were glad to see me again. Captain Kerr at first seeing me, asked me if I was not afraid to let him know who I was? and endeavoured to frighten me; yet his conduct towards me was humane and kind.—It had been very sickly on board the Princess-Royal, and the greater part of the hands which came out of England in her had died, and she was now manned chiefly with lascars, (country born people): among those who had died was the boatswain and the boatswain's mate, and Captain Kerr made me boatswain of the ship—in which office I continued until we arrived in London—and it protected me from being impressed at our arrival in England.

We sailed from St. Helena about the first of November, 1781, under convoy of the Experiment of 50 guns,* commanded by Captain Henry, and the Shark sloop of war of 18 guns (31)—and we arrived in London about the first of March, 1782,—it having been about two years and a half from the time I had left it.

In about a fortnight after our arrival in London,

---

* There is a mistake here. The Experiment of 50 guns was taken by the French, Sept. 24, 1779, when under the command of Sir James Wallace. Her successor, a 44 gun-ship, was not launched until 1784. The ship the writer alludes to was the Renown, of 50 guns, Capt. John Henry. For account of her see note (30).

I entered on board the King-George, (32) store-ship bound to Antigua, and after four weeks passage arrived there—the second night after we came to anchor in Antigua, I took the ship's boat and made my escape in her to Montserrat,* which place had but just before been taken by the French.—Here I did not meet with the treatment which I expected; for on my arrival at Montserrat I was immediately taken up and put in prison, where I continued 24 hours, and my boat taken from me;—I was then sent to Guadaloupe,† and examined by the governor.—I made known my case to him, by acquainting him with the misfortunes I had gone through in my captivity and in making my escape—he seemed to commiserate me—gave me ten dollars for the boat that I escaped in, and provided a passage for me on board a French brigantine‡ that was bound from

---

* The Isle of Montserrat in the West Indies, was discovered by Columbus in 1493, and was planted by England in 1632. It was taken by the French, Feb. 18, 1782, and was restored to England in 1783.

† One of the West India Islands, Leeward Group. The Governor at this time was Capt. Gen. Thomas Shirley.

‡ This was a small, flat, open, light vessel, going both with sails and oars, being intended either for fighting or giving

Guadaloupe to Philadelphia:—the vessel sailed in a few days—and now my prospects were favourable—but my misfortunes were not to end here; for after being out 21 days, we fell in with the Amphitrite (23) and Amphene, (24) two British cruizers, off the Capes of Delaware, by whom we were taken, carried into New-York, and put on board the Jersey (25) prison-ship—after being on board about a week, a cartel was fitted out for France, and I was sent on board as a French prisoner:—The cartel was ordered for St. Malo's,* and after a passage of 32 days we arrived safe at that place.

Finding no American vessel at St. Malo's, I went to the commandant and procured a pass to go by land to Port l'Orient;† on my arrival there I found three American privateers belonging to Beverley,‡ in the Massachusetts. I was much elated at seeing so many of my country, some of whom I was well

chase. These vessels were first used by pirates. The English brigantine was quite different; in fact, the term was variously applied by the mariners of different European nations.

* A seaport town in France.

† A seaport town in France.

‡ Beverly, a post town in Essex Co., Mass. First settled, 1626. Population in 1860, 6,154.

acquainted with. I immediately entered on board the Bucaneer—Captain Phierson:—We sailed on a cruize, and after being out 18 days, we returned to L'Orient with six prizes.—Three days after our arrival in port we heard the joyful news of peace;—on which the privateer was dismantled, the people discharged, and Capt. Phierson sailed on a merchant voyage to Norway.

I then entered on board a brig bound to Lisbon, (Capt. Ellenwood(36) of Beverly), and arrived at Lisbon in eight days—we took in a cargo of salt, and sailed for Beverly, where we arrived the 9th of May, 1783,—being now only 15 miles from home.—I immediately set for Cape-Ann,(37) went to my father's(38) house, and had an agreeable meeting with my friends, after an absence of almost six years.

New-London May 10, 1788.

JOHN BLATCHFORD(39).

[N. B. *Those who are acquainted with the narrator will not scruple to give full credit to the foregoing account—and others may satisfy themselves by conversing with him. The scars he carries are proof of a part of his narrative—and a gentleman belonging to New-London, who was several months with him, was acquainted with part of his sufferings, tho' it was out of his power to relieve him.—He is a poor man, with a wife and two children—His employment fishing and coasting.*]

BOSTON, *Dec.* 6. 1864.

I have carefully compared the foregoing copy (40 pages) with the printed tract in the Library of the Mass. Hist. Society, and hereby certify that it is an accurate transcript of the same.

J. APPLETON,

Assist't. Lib'n.

NOTES.

(1) The HANCOCK was one of the thirteen vessels authorized to be built by resolution of Congress of Dec. 13th, 1775, and was one of the two frigates which, by that resolve, were ordered to be constructed in Massachusetts. She mounted 32 twelve-pounder guns, and was built at, or near Boston, in 1776. As soon as she was equipped and ready for sea, she was placed under the command of Captain John Manly, and soon after sailed on a cruise. On the 27th day of June, 1777, in company with the frigate Boston, of 24 guns, she took off the coast of New Foundland, the British frigate Fox, of 28 guns, after an action of about two hours' duration. On the 8th day of July following, after a chase of more than 30 hours, the Hancock was captured by the Rainbow, of 44 guns, commanded by Sir George Collier, and taken to Halifax. Capt. Manly is thought to have lost her in consequence of having put her out of trim by starting the water in her fore hold. She was subsequently purchased on behalf of the British government, and added to the navy under the name of the Iris.

On the 7th day of June, 1780, while under the command of Capt. James Hawker, she encountered off the coast of North America, the French 36-gun frigate Hermoine, M. la Fouche Treville, commander, and after a severe action of one hour and twenty minutes, the latter was compelled to sheer off. On the 16th day of March, 1781, being then under the orders of Capt. George Dawson, the Iris formed one of the squadron under Admiral Arbuthnot in the action off the Chesapeake, with the squadron under M. de Ternay. On the 9th of August following, while cruising off the capes of Delaware, she fell in with the American ship Trumbull, of 28 guns, Capt. James Nicholson. A sharp action commenced, and continued for over an hour with no definite result, when another British frigate came up, whereupon, the Trumbull struck her colors. In this engagement the Trumbull had four men killed and five wounded, and the Iris one killed and six wounded. Previous to the contest the Trumbull had lost her fore-top mast in a gale of wind. She was a valuable prize, having five hundred barrels of fresh Philadelphia flour and bread on board. On the 10th day of September following, the Iris was sent to cut away the French buoys at the anchorage ground near the Chesapeake Bay, when she was intercepted and captured by the French squadron under M. de Barras. She was subsequently added to the French navy under the same name. During the time she was held by the British, she proved herself one of the fastest ships on the American station, and captured so many rich prizes, that she is said to have made the fortunes of all who commanded her. Her place in the British service was supplied by another frigate, of the same name and force, which was built on the river Thames in 1783. The Iris remained in the possession of the French until the year 1793, when she was blown up at Toulon, as a magazine, by the Spaniards.

(₂) Capt. JOHN MANLY was a native of Massachusetts, and was born in the year 1733. After receiving the rudiments of education, he embraced the maritime life, and soon became noted for his energy and professional merit. In 1775 he commanded the schooner Lee, and in November of that year, took the Nancy, a transport bound to Boston, and laden with valuable munitions of war, of which the colonists were then in great need. While in this command he made other valuable prizes, one of which he captured in sight of the British fleet in Boston harbor. His zeal and enterprise attracted the attention of Congress, and that body, in the following year, appointed him a captain in the navy, and gave him the command of the Hancock, a beautiful frigate of 32 guns, then building in Massachusetts. In this vessel he captured the Fox, June 27th, 1777, and in July following this prize was retaken by the Flora of 32 guns, Capt. Brisbane. About the same time, the Hancock struck to the Rainbow, Sir George Collier, after a long chase, and was taken with her crew to Halifax. In a few days after, Capt. Manly was conveyed to New York, where he remained a prisoner until the month of April of the year following. He was then released and returned to Boston, when his conduct was investigated, but the result of the inquiry left him without reproach. Soon after this he was put in command of the Cumberland, a new privateer of 20 guns, and in Jan., 1779, while cruising in her off the southern coast, was taken by the Pomona frigate of 28 guns, Capt. Waldegrave, and carried into Barbadoes, where he and his officers were imprisoned. Finding that their applications for paroles were rejected, they determined to attempt their escape. This they effected by taking possession of a Bermudian sloop, and steering their course for Martinico, where they arrived in safety and sold their vessel. On his return home, Capt. Manly was appointed to the privateer Jason, of 20 guns, which vessel had just before been taken from the British. On the 25th July, 1779, while on a cruise in her, he was attacked by two British privateers, one of 18 and the other of 16 guns. Reserving his fire, Capt. Manly ran between the privateers, and poured his starboard broadside into one, and his larboard broadside into the other with great effect, whereupon both his opponents struck their colors. In the month of August following, while cruising off the coast of Nova Scotia, he took a ship of 14 guns, and 20 men. In November, after an obstinate engagement of four glasses, Capt. Manly was captured by the Perseus frigate of 20 guns. In this contest the Jason lost 18 killed and 12 wounded, and the Perseus 7 killed and 10 wounded. Having been exchanged, Capt. Manly was on the 11th Sept., 1782, appointed to the frigate Hague, formerly the

Deane, of 32 guns, and sailed for the West Indies. A few days after leaving Martinique, he was descried by a British 74, and to avoid capture, he ran his ship on a sand bank near Guadaloupe. While thus exposed, he is said to have sustained the fire from the enemy's ships for three days with undaunted firmness. On the 4th he got off, when, hoisting his colors at the main-top-gallant-mast, and firing 13 guns in farewell defiance, he made his escape and arrived safely in Boston, where, this exploit having gained him much eclat, he was received with marked attention. Capt. Manly continued in command of the Hague, and his ship was one of the last cruisers at sea in the war. She was frequently chased, and made many narrow escapes. After the peace, Capt. Manly returned to Boston, and retired to private life. He died in that city, Feb. 12, 1793, in the 60th year of his age.

(₃) The Fox was a British frigate mounting 28 guns, four of which were four-pounders, and the remaining twenty-four long nine-pounders. She was registered as a sixth-rate, and was built on the river Thames in the year 1774. She was placed under the command of Capt. P. Fotheringham, and in 1776 formed one of the squadron at New Foundland, under John Montagu, vice-admiral of the white. On the 27th day of June, 1777, while on a cruise near the Banks of New Foundland, she fell in with the American frigates Hancock, of 32 guns, and Boston, of 24 guns. An action commenced and continued for about two hours. During the engagement the Fox took fire in the main chains, where a number of wads had been deposited. Upon this, the Americans ceased firing until the flames were extinguished, when the contest was resumed. The Fox being at length reduced to a wreck, and having sustained a severe loss in killed and wounded, Capt. Fotheringham ordered the colors to be hauled down. The Lieut. of Marines, Hon. James J. Napier, was among the wounded. In July following, while the prize was being conveyed by her captors to Boston, the British ship Rainbow hove in sight and gave chase to the Hancock, while the Boston effected her escape. During the chase, the 32-gun frigate Flora came up and recaptured the Fox, and carried her into Halifax. The Fox, after undergoing repairs, was again taken into the British service. She was placed under the orders of Hon. Thomas Windsor, manned with a crew of 200 men, and in 1778, formed one of the fleet of Admiral Keppel, which in July of that year was cruising off Brest in search of the French fleet under Comte d' Orvilliers. On the 10th of September following, while off the French coast, she was chased by the 34-gun frigate Junon, commanded by Vicomte de Beaumont. The weather being thick and hazy, the Junon was not perceived until close aboard of the Fox, when the latter hove to and awaited the approach of the Frenchman. An action commenced, and lasted for three hours, when the Fox, being totally dismasted, having several guns disabled, 11 men killed, and Capt. Windsor and 49 of his men wounded, many of them mortally, hauled down her colors. The Junon had a crew of

330 men, and carried six 6-pounders and 28 long twelves. The Fox was succeeded in the British navy by a 32-gun frigate of the same name, of 697 tons burden, built at Bursledon, in the year 1780.

PATRICK FOTHERINGHAM was made lieut. on the 13th day of Dec., 1760, promoted to commander April 1, 1765, and raised to the rank of captain, Sept. 2, 1773. About the year 1772, he was appointed to the sloop Merlin, of 18 guns, in which vessel he seems to have served until 1775, when he was made capt. of the Fox, of 28 guns, and soon after, ordered to North America. Capt. Fotheringham was tried by court-martial at Portsmouth, March 3, 1778, for the loss of his ship, and he and his officers were honorably acquitted. He was soon after appointed to the Resource, of 28 guns, in which frigate he remained for the usual period. He died in the West Indies in the spring of 1781, while captain of the ship Ruby.

(*) The RAINBOW was registered as a fifth-rate, carried 44 guns, and was built on the river Thames in 1761, to succeed a 40-gun ship of the same name, then broken up. The dimensions of our vessel were as follows: length of gun-deck, 131 feet 3 in.; of keel, 108 ft. 3½ in.; breadth, 37 ft. 10¾ in.; depth in hold, 16 ft.; tons, 831. In the year 1762, she was placed under the orders of Capt. Mark Robinson, and formed one of the Havanna squadron under Commodore Elliot, at which time she carried a crew of 380 men. In 1764 she was commanded by Capt. Walter Sterling, and was on duty in

North America. She remained on this station till 1766, when she returned home and was put out of commission. A short time after the prospect of a rupture with Spain had passed away, Capt. Charles Fielding was appointed to the Rainbow, then equipping for service at Chatham, a command which he retained for nearly two years. Towards the conclusion of 1771, Thomas Collingwood was placed in command of her, and he seems to have remained in her for the usual period of three years, doing duty a part of the time on the coast of Guinea. At the commencement of the dispute with the North American colonies, she was placed under the orders of Sir George Collier, and came to America with Commodore Hotham, and a large re-inforcement of troops for the army under Gen. Howe. In 1776 she co-operated with the army in the reduction of New York, and in 1777 she was stationed at Halifax, where she was one of a small squadron employed in protecting the fisheries as well as the trade in that quarter. In the month of July, being on a cruise, she fell in with, and after a long chase, captured the Hancock frigate of 32 guns and 290 men—a ship esteemed at that time the finest in the American service, and one of the fastest sailing vessels ever built. After this, the Rainbow proceeded to Machias, and along the coast of New England, burning the vessels and destroying the stores intended for the contemplated invasion by the Americans of Nova Scotia. In the beginning of 1779 she was one of a squadron that sailed from New York in company with transports conveying troops under Gen. Matthew to Hampton Roads, and she co-operated with the army in the reduction of Norfolk, Suffolk, Portsmouth, and Gosport. A short time after this, John Kendall was appointed to her, and shortly after, she returned home and went into dock at Chatham. Having been thoroughly overhauled, she was placed under the orders of Henry Trollope, and sailed on the 2d day of Sept., 1782, for Plymouth, to join Commodore Elliot in the Channel. When off the Isle of Bas, she fell in with and captured the French frigate La Hebe, of 40 guns and 360 men, then on her way from St. Malo to Brest, with a convoy, which in the chase, being close in shore, got into Morlais in safety. In the engagement, the Rainbow lost only one man, while her opponent had her 2d capt. and four men killed, besides several wounded. Among the latter was Mons. de Vigny, the commander of the French vessel. The Hebe being a fine ship, was purchased by government, and added to the Royal navy under the same name. This action appears to have been the last active service of the Rainbow, for we find her in 1784 reported as a hulk. Shortly after this she was fitted up as a receiving ship, and stationed at Woolwich. She was used in this capacity until about the year 1801, when she was broken up. The "Rainbow" seems to have been a favorite name in the British navy, as we read of one as early as 1594, in a squadron under Sir Martin Frobisher, sent to aid the French in their attack upon Brest, which was then in possession of the Spaniards.

SIR GEORGE COLLIER was born in 1738. He entered the

navy when about thirteen years of age, and served part of his time with Sir George Pocock. He was made commander, Aug. 6, 1761, and attained the rank of captain, July 12, 1762. About this time, he was appointed to the Bologne, of 32 guns, in which vessel he served till the following year, when peace having taken place, he was appointed to the Edgar, of 60 guns, then a guard-ship at Plymouth. In 1770, he was commissioned to the Tweed frigate, and sailed on a cruise in the Channel in a small squadron under the Duke of Cumberland. He subsequently commanded the Levant, of 28 guns, and afterwards the Flora, of 32, and in 1775, received the honor of knighthood. About this time he was appointed to the Rainbow, of 44 guns, and in 1776, proceeded in her to North America. He assisted in the reduction of New York in that year, and in 1777, commanded the detachment of the fleet stationed at Halifax, distinguishing himself greatly by his energy and activity. In July he captured the American frigate Hancock, of 32 guns, and soon after bringing her into port, he proceeded to Machias, where he destroyed the magazines and storehouses filled with flour, rice and other articles, which the Americans had collected there for a contemplated invasion of Nova Scotia, and subsequently burnt 30 sail of vessels along the coast of New England. He continued on that station till March, 1779, when he moved into the Raisonable of 64 guns, on board of which he hoisted his broad pendant as commander-in-chief, pro tempore, on the American station. In May following, he commanded the fleet in the expedition to Virginia, and in conjunction with a land force under Gen. Matthew, took possession of Portsmouth, Norfolk, Gosport and Suffolk, capturing a large quantity of stores, cannon and ammunition, and destroying many vessels and much property of all kind. After his return to New York, he assisted in the reduction of Stony Point, Fort Lafayette and Verplanck's Point, subsequently co-operated with Gen. Tryon in the destruction of Norwalk, Fairfield and Greenfield, and in July following went to the relief of Penobscot, where he signally defeated the American fleet under Saltonstall, capturing and destroying the whole force, amounting to 37 large armed vessels. After this he returned to New York, where he found Admiral Arbuthnot, to whom he resigned the command of the squadron, and then returned to England. In 1780 he was appointed to the Canada, of 74 guns, one of the ships belonging to the Channel fleet; in the following year he accompanied Admiral Darby to the relief of Gibraltar, and in 1784 was elected M. P. for Honiton. In 1790, on the expectation of a rupture with Spain, he was appointed to the St. George, of 98 guns; but the dispute being accommodated, the St. George was paid off. On the 1st Feb., 1793, he was made rear-admiral of the white, on the 12th April, 1794, rear-admiral of the red, and on the 12th July following, vice-admiral of the white, which was the highest rank he lived to attain. In Jan., 1795, he was appointed to the chief command at the Nore, but was compelled to resign on account of ill health. He died on the 6th day of April following. Sir George had blue eyes, light hair, and fair complexion. Though of medium height, he was well proportioned and very active. As a private individual, he was amiable and benevolent, sociable and pleasant; as an officer, brave, active and persevering, cool and determined in battle, slow to punish, but a strict observer of discipline. He was possessed of much literary taste, and was the translator of Selima and Azor, a dramatic romance, which was successfully performed at Drury Lane Theatre in 1776. He was twice married. His first wife was Miss Christiana Gwyn, to whom he was united in 1773. By her he had one son. His second wife was Miss Elizabeth Fryer, to whom he was married in 1781. By her he had two daughters and four sons. The latter all entered the service of their country—two in the army and two in the navy. George, the eldest of the four, became lieutenant-colonel of the Coldstream Guards, and was killed in his 31st year in the sortie from Bayonne, March 10, 1814.

(*s*) The FLORA was a fifth-rate British frigate, mounting 32 guns. She was formerly the Vestale French frigate of 32 guns, and was captured off the French coast on the 8th January, 1761, by the Union frigate of 28 guns, Capt. Joseph Hunt, after a severe action, in which Capt. Hunt was killed, and M. Boisbertelot, the commander of the Vestale, had his leg shot off, in consequence of which he died the next day. The Vestale was repaired and added to the British navy, under the name of the Flora. In 1762 she was stationed in the

Downs, and was then commanded by Capt. Gamaliel Nightingale. She remained on home duty but a short time, as peace took place soon after, and she was then put out of commission. Her next employment appears to have been in 1773, at which time she was commanded by Capt. George Collier, and was on the home station. Soon after the commencement of the contest with the colonies, Capt. John Brisbane was appointed to her, and in 1776 she was ordered to North America with a convoy. She was employed here subsequently on a variety of desultory service. In July, 1777, she re-captured the Fox, a frigate of 28 guns, which had been taken on the Banks of New Foundland, a short time before, by the American frigates Hancock and Boston. In the summer of 1778, she was one of the small squadron under Capt. Brisbane, that was stationed off Rhode Island, to protect that post and distress the commerce of the neighboring coast. While thus employed, the French fleet, under Comte d'Estaing, comprising 12 ships of the line and 4 frigates, made its appearance off Rhode Island on the 28th of July, and after several previous indications of attack in less force, entered the harbor of Newport on the 8th day of August following. In consequence of this, the officers of Capt. Brisbane's squadron, then lying in the harbor, were reduced to the necessity of burning or sinking their ships, to prevent them from falling into the hands of the enemy, and the Flora was one of those that were sunk. Her place in the British navy was supplied by a 36-gun frigate, of the same name, which was built at Deptford in the year 1780, and which, after serving with distinction, was lost on the 18th January, 1808, by striking upon Schelling Reef. The 32-gun frigate Flora, the subject of our sketch, after being submerged for some time, was at length weighed by the Americans, and sold by them to the French, who gave her the name of the Flore. On the 7th September, 1798, she was captured off the French coast, after a long chase, by the Phaëton frigate of 38 guns, Hon. Robert Stopford, and the Anson frigate of 44 guns, Philip C. Durham. Her subsequent history we have been unable to learn further than that she was sold soon after she was brought into port.

JOHN BRISBANE was appointed lieutenant, Aug. 5, 1757, and was raised to the rank of captain on the 24th Sept., 1760. For a short time he commanded the Nightingale, a 20-gun ship, on the American station. After this he was appointed to the Echo, a 24-gun frigate, lately taken from the French, and was ordered to the West Indies. He continued there till the end of the war, when he returned home, and his ship was put out of commission. In 1769 he was appointed to the Ceberus, of 28 guns, and after being in her a short time, he returned to Chatham, when his ship was laid up. Soon after the commencement of the American revolution, he was appointed to the Flora, of 32 guns, and in 1776 sailed in her to America, where he had been ordered with a convoy. In July, 1777, he recaptured the Fox frigate of 28 guns, and in the summer of the following year, was stationed off Rhode

Island as senior or commanding officer of a small squadron. Having lost his ship while in this command, he returned home in the fall, when he was appointed to the Alcide, a new ship of 74 guns. In December, 1779, he sailed with Sir George Rodney to Gibraltar, but was not materially, if at all, engaged in the action with the Spanish squadron. He subsequently proceeded to the West Indies, and thence to America, after which he was sent home by Sir George Rodney, with the information of that officer's arrival on the American station with the West India detachment. He reached England in December, and then quitted the command of the Alcide. In the ensuing year he was appointed to the Hercules, of the same force, but in consequence of impaired health, he was under the necessity of resigning this command in December following. On the 21st September, 1790, he was made rear-admiral of the blue, and on the 12th April, 1794, was advanced to vice-admiral of the blue. On the 4th July following, he was raised to vice-admiral of the white, and on the 1st June, 1795, was advanced to vice-admiral of the red. He died on the 10th December, 1807. He had by his wife, Mary, two daughters and also six sons, three of whom died in the service of their country. The widow of Admiral Brisbane died at Brighton, April 29th, 1817.

(₆) The CABOT was a brig of 189 tons burden, mounted 14 guns, believed to be six-pounders, and was purchased by Congress in 1775. On the 22d December of that year, the command of her was given to Capt. John B. Hopkins, and in February following, she formed one of the squadron under Commodore Ezek Hopkins, in his attack upon New Providence. On her return she engaged the Glasgow frigate of 20 guns, Capt. Tyringham Howe; but the latter being too heavy a force for her, she was compelled to sheer off, having her captain wounded, her master killed, and a number of her crew injured. She was subsequently placed under the command of Capt. Elisha Hinman, and in the month of October she took two ships from Jamaica bound to London, with sugar, rum and indigo, five ships and a brig, all from Jamaica, one of them a 3-decker, with upwards of 600 hhds. on board. Her next commander was Capt. Joseph Olney. While under his orders, in March, 1777, she was chased on shore on the coast of Nova Scotia by the British frigate Milford, of 28 guns, Capt. John Burr, (see Allen's Battles Brit. Navy, vol. i., p. 242,) who pressed her so hard that she had barely time to get her people out. Capt. Olney and crew, after abandoning their vessel, retreated to the woods, and subsequently seized a schooner, in which they got home in safety. The enemy, after a long trial, got the Cabot off. She was taken into the British service, under the same name, and placed under the command of Edward Dodd. On the 13th May, 1779, she was one of the squadron of Sir James Wallace that drove a division of the French force in Cancale Bay, in which service she had her purser killed and two of her men wounded. In 1780 she was under the command of Henry

Cromwell, and was one of the squadron of Vice-admiral Parker, in the battle with the Dutch squadron under Rear-admiral Zoutman, off the Dogger Bank, on the 5th day of August of the following year. In 1782 she was at Sheerness, and she appears to have been broken up or otherwise disposed of shortly afterwards.

CAPT. JOSEPH OLNEY was, we believe, a native of Rhode Island. In 1752 he was one of five citizens of Providence who were appointed to have the care of the town school-house. Previous to the Revolution, he kept for many years the principal public house in Providence. On the 22d December, 1775, he was appointed by Congress a lieutenant, and on the 10th October, 1776, was promoted to the rank of captain. He does not appear to have had any command after the loss of the Cabot. He probably retired to Providence and died there.

(₇) The MILFORD was registered as a sixth-rate, carried 28 guns, and was built in 1759. In 1762 she was commanded by Robert Mann, 2d, and on the 7th day of March, when on a cruise in the bay, she fell in with and engaged the letter-of-marque La Gloire, from Bordeaux, bound to St. Domingo, pierced for 20 guns, but had only 16 six-pounders, and 10 swivels mounted, with a crew of 94 men. Capt. Mann receiving a mortal wound in the early part of the action, the command devolved upon Lieut. Day, who fought his ship with great bravery, until he fell severely wounded. His place was then supplied by Lieut. Nash, who continued the engagement with spirit, and at length compelled his opponent to strike his colors. The La Gloire lost her mainmast in the action, had her rigging, sails and hull cut to pieces, and 6 of her crew killed and 18 wounded. The Milford, beside her captain and first-lieutenant, had 2 killed and 13 wounded. In 1763 the Milford was commanded by Capt. J. Reynolds, and was in service on the coast of Africa; in 1766 Thomas Cornwell was appointed to her, and in 1770 she was at Woolwich, probably undergoing repair. In the year 1775 Captain John Burr was appointed to command her, and in 1776 she came to America. In the month of June following, while cruising off Cape Ann, she fell in with and captured the American privateer Yankee Hero, commanded by Captain Tracy, of Newburyport, after a severe engagement of nearly two glasses. In the contest the Yankee Hero had four of her crew killed and fourteen wounded. Capt. Tracy was wounded in the leg. Lieutenant Main was badly injured, and Mr. Rowe, of Cape Ann, sustained the loss of an arm. In the month of September, while on a cruise off Cape Sable, the Milford fell in with the Providence, of 28 guns, commanded by Captain Paul Jones. An engagement ensued, and continued for several hours, when her opponent was compelled to sheer off. At the close of the year she fell in with the Alfred, of 28 guns, to which vessel Capt. Jones had recently been appointed. An action took place and lasted for some time, when the Alfred, availing herself of a hard gust of wind which arose, succeeded in effecting her escape. In March, 1777, the Milford chased the 14-gun brig Cabot, Capt. Joseph Olney, ashore on the coast of Nova Scotia, and in June, 1778, being then under the orders of Sir Wm. Burnaby, and attached to the fleet off Brest under Admiral Keppel, she, in company with another vessel, compelled the French frigate Licorne, of 32 guns, to haul down her colors. In August, 1779, she was one of the Channel fleet under Sir Charles Hardy, and was attached to the centre division in line of battle. In 1780, Capt. Philip Patton was appointed to her, and under him she formed one of the Channel fleet in Torbay, under command of Vice-admiral George Darby. Having become leaky and in need of great repair, Capt. Patton quitted her, and she was soon after broken up. Her place in the navy was supplied by a 74-gun ship, which we find building in the year 1799.

JOHN BURR, who we believe commanded this frigate at the time referred to in the narrative, was made lieutenant in the year 1758; raised to commander, Sept. 13, 1769, and promoted to the rank of captain on the 15th day of October, 1773. In 1770 he commanded the sloop Hound, of 14 guns, and in 1775 was appointed to the Milford frigate, of 28 guns, which appears to have been his last command. He died (says Schomberg, vol. v., p. 346) in the year 1784.

(*) The following particulars we take from the papers of the day:

"HALIFAX, July 12.

This Day arrived his Majesty's Ship Rainbow, *Sir* George Collier, *having brought into this Harbour, the* HANCOCK *Frigate, commanded by Mr.* Manley; *the following are some Particulars relative to the meeting the* Rebel Squadron under Manley, *by his Majesty's Ship Rainbow, commanded by Sir* George Collier.

ON Sunday the 6th July, at Half past 4 in the Afternoon (Cape Sambro' then bearing N. E. about 12 or 13 Leagues) we discovered three Sail from the Mast-head, which we immediately gave chace to, but from the Distance could form no Judgment of their Force, or what they were; the Victor Brig was at this Time in Company, three or four Miles astern, and as her Rate of sailing was much inferior to that of the Rainbow, we made Signal for her to make more Sail, being apprehensive otherwise of separating from her; at Sun-set we had gained so much on the Chace, as to discover they were large Ships, standing as we were close on a Wind, which was at W. N. W., and seemed to us a conclusive Proof that they were bound to some of the Ports in New-England; we continued the Chace, and at Dawn of Day in the Morning saw them again about three Points on the Weather-Bow, with a Sloop in Company: the prest Sail we had carried all Night, had encreased the Distance from the Victor Brig so much, that she was no longer discernable from the Mast-head:—The

Ships we were in Chace of, were about five or six Miles distant, and from many Circumstances we had no doubt were part of the Rebel Fleet, who had sailed some Time before from Boston under the command of Mr. Manley; continuing the Chace, and gaining upon them, they quitted their Prize Sloop and set her on Fire, going off in a regular Line of Battle-a-head, and setting Top-gallant Royals, and every Sail that could be useful to them.

A little after six A. M. another Sail was discovered, standing towards the Rebel Ships; she crossed us on the contrary Tack, at about four Miles Distance; and put about, when she could fetch their Wakes; from her not making the *private Signal*, we had no doubt but that she was another of the Rebel Frigates, and therefore, *Sir George* paid no Regard to an English red Ensign she hoisted, and two Guns she fired to the Leeward.

About Ten in the Morning, the Enemy's Ships went away lasking; and three Quarters of an Hour afterwards, we were surprized to see several Shot exchanged between the Sternmost of them, and the Stranger who had last joined, and whom we had hitherto looked upon as another of their Fleet; we then hoisted our Colours, and soon afterwards the two Sternmost of the Rebel Frigates hawled their Wind, whilst the Headmost kept away about two Points from it; this brought the English Ship (which we afterwards found to be the Flora) more a breast of them, and she passed them to the Windward, exchanging a Broadside with each, and pursuing the Fugitive, who from the Alteration two or three Times of her Course, seemed uncertain which to steer: The Flora gained fast upon her, which she perceiving, hawled her Wind again, and soon afterwards tacked and stood after her Comrades, exchanging a Broad-side with the Flora as they passed each other.

We were just putting about after the two Ships, when we observed this, which made us stand on something longer, before we tacked, hoping to get her within reach of our Guns as she passed us: We accordingly did so, but had not the good Fortune to bring down either a Mast or Sail by our Fire.

We tacked immediately after her, and soon afterwards saw the head-most Rebel Frigate put about, and pass us just out of Gun-shot to Windward; she appeared a very fine Ship of 34 Guns and had Rebel Colours flying; one of the Gentlemen on the Quarter Deck had been a Prisoner lately at Boston, and knew her to be the *Hancock*, on board of whom *Manley* commanded, who is the second in Rank in the Rebel Army.*

The Ship we had fired upon, out sail'd us fast; and soon after our tacking kept away lasking; whilst the other Frigate standing as we did, kept her Wind; we then found that one of the three must unavoidably escape, if they steered thus, different Courses; *Sir George* therefore judg'd it best to put about after the *Hancock*, who appeared the largest Ship, the Rainbow, passed the Flora very near, who continued pursuing the Ship we had fired upon.

* Intended for *Navy*.—Ed.

It was about two o'Clock in the Afternoon (of Monday the 7th of July) that we tack'd after Mr. Manley, who seem'd at first rather to out-sail the Rainbow, but we understood afterwards that to endeavour making her sail better, he started his Water forward, and by that Means put her out of Trim: An Hour before the close of Day, he altered his Course, and kept away large, we however got so near to him before Dark, as enabled us (by Means of a Night Glass) to keep Sight of him all Night:—At Dawn of Day she was not much more than a Mile ahead of us, soon after which we saw a small Sail to Leeward, which we found to be the Victor Brig, who as we pass'd fired into the Rebel Frigate and killed one of the Men at the Wheel, but was not able for bad sailing to keep up or come near any more. About four in the Morning we began firing the Bow Chace upon her, with occasioned Broadsides loaded with round and Grape, as we could bring them to bear, some of which struck her Masts and Sails. At half past eight we were so near as to hail her, and acquaint them that if they expected Quarters, they must strike immediately; Manley took a few Minutes to consider, and a fresher Breeze just then springing up, he availed himself of it, by attempting to set some of the steering sails on the other side, we therefore poured a Number of Shot into him which brought him to the expected Determination, and he struck the Rebel Colours a little before 9 o'Clock in the Morning, after a Chace of upwards of 30 Hours.

We immediately took Possession of her, and sent Part of the

Prisoners on board the Rainbow; she prov'd to be the Hancock of 34 Guns, 12 Pounders, and had upwards of 229 Men on board; she is a very capital and large Frigate, is quite new of the Stocks, and tho' from her Foulness and their Mismanagement we came up with her, yet we are informed that she is one of the fastest sailing Ships ever built.

The Prisoners inform'd us that the Ship the Flora was in Chase of, was his Majesty's Ship the Fox, of 28 Guns, which Manley had lately taken on the Banks of New Foundland, after a close and very warm Action of two Hours; the other Frigate was the Boston, of 30 Guns, commanded by McNeill... Capt. Fotheringham of the Fox, and 40 of his People were on board the Hancock, but his Officers and some other of the Men were on board the Boston Frigate, and the Remainder ashore at New Foundland.

After exchanging the Prisoners we found it necessary from their Number being almost as many as our own Ship's Company, to return to this Port.

Manley seem'd much chagrin'd at his not having engaged the Rainbow, when he found she was but a 40 Gun Ship, as he had all along mistaken her for the Raisonable, whom he knew was very lately at Louisbourg.

We hear the Prize Sloop which the Rebel Fleet set Fire to when chac'd by the Rainbow, was call'd the Brittania, and laden with coals from Louisbourg for Halifax, Hinxman, Master."

Gaine, Mon: Aug: 4, 1777. No. 1345.

"NEW-YORK, August 4.

Wednesday last the Syren Frigate arrived here from Halifax, and has brought Capt. Fotheringham of the Fox, and about 40 of his Seamen, with Captain Manley and his first Lieut. the latter commanded the Fox when taken by the Flora. We hear Mr. Manley is on board the St. Albans.

A letter from Halifax, dated the 13th of July, says, " The public Prints will inform you of the retaking of the Fox Frigate, by the Flora, Capt. Brisbane, as also the taking of the Hancock, Manley, by the Rainbow."

Gaine, Mon: Aug: 4, 1777. No. 1345.

"BOSTON, April 23.

Last Tuesday arrived in town from New-York, where he has long been held a prisoner, the brave John Manley Esq. late Commander of the Continental Frigate Hancock."

Holt's N. Y. Journal, Mon. May 19, 1778.

See also
Compilation by G. S. Ranier from Official Papers, Brit. Naval Chronicle, Vol: 32, pp. 266–400. "Detail of Particular Services, &c." pub: by Ithiel Town, N. Y., 1835.
Allen's Battles British Navy, vol. i. pp: 212–244.

(9) HALIFAX, the capital of Nova Scotia, was settled in 1748. It was originally called Chebucto, and received the name of Halifax, in honor of Lord Halifax, a member of the British ministry. The city is on the west side of Halifax harbor, and on the declivity of a commanding hill. Its appearance in 1760 is thus described by Alex. Grant, in a

letter to Rev. Dr. Stiles, dated Halifax, May, 1760, (see Mass. Hist. Collec., 1st series, vol. x., p. 79.) "This place is divided into three towns—Halifax, Irishtown, and Dutchtown. The whole may contain about 1,000 houses, great and small, many of which are employed as barracks, hospitals for the army and navy, and other publick uses. The inhabitants may be about three thousand, one-third of which are Irish, and many of them Roman Catholicks; and about one-fourth Germans and Dutch, the most industrious and useful settlers among us; and the rest English, with a very small number of Scotch. We have upwards of one hundred licenced houses, and perhaps as many more which retail spirituous liquors without licence; so that the business of one-half of the town is to sell rum, and of the other half to drink it."

The city, at the present day, is about two miles in length, is well laid out in oblong squares, the streets parallel, and at right angles. Many of the houses are of wood, plastered and stuccoed, but many also are handsomely built of stone. The public buildings are substantial structures. The population in 1852 was 26,000, and the total value of exports $2,846,917.

Queen's Slip, formerly called Governor's Slip, is on the east side of the city, near the centre of the original town. Here the Governors, on their arrival from Europe, usually landed. They were here received by the Council, etc., and were thence escorted to the Council Chamber, to be publicly sworn into office. Hence arose its name "*Governor's Slip.*"

(10) Through the courtesy of M. M. Jackson, Esq., U. S. Consul at Halifax, the following particulars, furnished by Beamish Murdock, Esq., the Historian of Nova Scotia, have been placed at our command :

"On the west or upper side of Hollis street, not far from the Halifax Hotel, there is an old wooden building, now in ruins, which is known as the *Old Jail*," in which Ethan Allen, Hon. Jas. Lovell and others are said to have been confined, and which is thought to have been the building alluded to in the text. "This building, as originally built, was a long, one-story house, with a sharp pitched roof, running perhaps 50 to 60 feet in length from the street to the end of the lot. It stood on a rough kind of stone wall which elevated it a few feet, (perhaps six feet) above the ground, and steps were attached to the building outside, not on the street, but within the enclosure. It was used as a prison not only during the Revolution but also in 1786. About 150 yards from the Jail, stood in the last century, a brick building built by Malachi Salter, which was at one time used as a Sugar House. It was situated at the corner of Salter and Pleasant streets. It is not known to have been used as a prison."

The following notices of the "*Old Jail*," we take from the papers of the day :

" BOSTON, September 1.

Our American Prisoners (to the Number of 31) are confined in the Common Gaol of Halifax (a lousy, filthy, unwholesome Place) and are treated in the most inhuman and barbarous Manner possible, having nothing to live upon but salt Provisions (and that very scanty) thrown in among Negroes, Robbers, &c., and are told, they know no distinction."

N. Hampshire Gazette, Sat., Aug. 3, 1776.

"SALEM, Jan. 10.

Since our last a cartel arrived from Halifax with upwards of 100 prisoners, many of them in a very emaciated, sickly condition. Five of the number which came out, died on the passage."

Pennsylvania Packet, Thurs., Feb. 7, 1782.

(11) The BOSTON was one of the 13 vessels authorized to be built by resolution of Congress of Dec. 13, 1775, and was one of the two frigates which were ordered by that resolve to be constructed in Massachusetts. She mounted 24 guns, and was launched at or near Boston in 1776. She was placed under the command of Capt. Hector McNeil, and soon after sailed on a cruise. She was in company with the Hancock in June, 1777, when the Fox frigate was taken, and also at the time when the Rainbow was first discovered, but made her escape without affording her comrade any assistance. After her return to port, she was placed under the command of Capt. Samuel Tucker, and continued under his orders as long as she remained in the American service. In the early part of 1778 she carried John Adams to France, he having been appointed a commissioner in place of Silas Deane, who had been recalled. On her way she captured three very valuable prizes, one of which, the Martha, was laden with bale goods to the amount, as was supposed, of £80,000. As Mr. Adams was upon urgent business, the Boston was not able to remain with her prize,

and it was subsequently retaken by the Rainbow. The Boston on her voyage made several narrow escapes from destruction. Among other dangers, she was struck by lightning, which shattered her mast and came very nigh blowing her up, the fire when extinguished having nearly reached the magazine of powder. She reached Bordeaux, however, on the 1st April, in safety, and in consequence of the treaties of commerce and alliance having been signed before the arrival of Mr. Adams, that gentleman soon returned in her to America. On the 9th Aug., 1779, the Boston, in company with the ship Deane, Capt. Samuel Nicholson, captured off the capes of Virginia, the ship Glencairn, from Glasgow, of 20 guns and 30 men; on the 12th took the Sandwich packet from New York, bound to Falmouth, Eng., of 16 guns and 60 men; on the 23d made a prize of the brigantine Venture, from Madeira, of 2 guns and 20 men; and on the 24th captured the Thorn, of 18 guns, but mounting only 14, and having a crew of 135 men. During the latter part of 1779 and the fore part of 1780, the Boston formed one of the squadron of Commodore Abraham Whipple, that cruised along the Southern coast, capturing a number of merchant vessels. While thus employed, she, with other American ships, on the appearance of the British fleet, put into Charleston, S. C., for safety, and on the surrender of the city, May 12, 1780, she was one of the vessels that were captured by the enemy.

CAPT. HECTOR McNEIL was appointed by Congress to the command of the Boston frigate, June 15, 1776. He was with

Capt. Manly at the taking of the Fox, but when the Rainbow and Flora hove in view, he sought his own safety in flight, rendering his companion no assistance whatever. A court-martial was shortly afterwards held upon his conduct, when being found guilty of cowardice, he was dismissed the service forthwith.

(12) This is not the only occasion when a deceased American prisoner was so interred. We give another instance, occurring much nearer home.

"On the 4th day of Feb., 1841, some workmen, while engaged in digging away an embankment in Jackson street, near the Navy Yard, accidentally discovered a quantity of human bones, among which, horrible to relate, was a skeleton, having a pair of *iron manacles still upon the wrists.*"

Thompson's Hist. of Long Island, vol. i., p. 244.

(13) The GREYHOUND was registered as a sixth-rate, carried 24 guns, and was built about the year 1775, as successor to a 20-gun ship which was broken up about that time. In the year 1776, our vessel was placed under the command of Capt. Archibald Dickson, and ordered to North America. She proceeded to Halifax, Nova Scotia, where she took General Howe on board as a passenger, and then sailed for New York, arriving at Sandy Hook on the 25th day of June. In the month of August following, she co-operated with the British army in the reduction of New York, and was one of the

frigates stationed in Gravesend Bay on the 22d of that month, to cover the landing of the troops. In 1779 she was one of the squadron of Sir George Collier, and in the month of August, assisted in the signal destruction of the American squadron, under Commodore Saltonstal, in Penobscot Bay, soon after which she returned to England with despatches. In the latter part of the year she composed one of the fleet of Sir George B. Rodney, in the West Indies, at which time she was under the orders of Capt. William Fookes, who was succeeded in command of her by Capt. William Fox. Under the latter officer the Greyhound was lost upon the South Sand Head in the year 1781. Her crew were saved. She was succeeded in the service by a 36-gun frigate of the same name, which we find building at Betts' Yard, in Mistleythorne, in the year 1783.

(14) ARCHIBALD DICKSON was made lieut., Sept. 19, 1759; commander, Jan. 10, 1771; and raised to rank of capt. in 1773. In 1776 he was appointed to the Greyhound frigate, and continued in her for the usual period. He carried home the particulars of the destruction of the American fleet in Penobscot Bay, and was presented by the British Admiralty with £500 for the intelligence he brought. In 1782 he commanded the Dublin, of 74 guns; in 1787 the Goliah, of the same force, then employed as a guard-ship; and in 1793 the Egmont, also of 74 guns. He was made rear-admiral of the white in 1794, vice-admiral of the blue in 1795, admiral of the blue in 1801, and April 13, 1802, was created a baronet. He died in the

spring of 1805. Sir Archibald Dickson, Bt., was the brother of William Dickson, admiral of the blue, who died in 1803.

(15) The VULTURE was a British sloop-of-war, carrying 14 guns, and was built about the year 1776. She was placed under the orders of James Feattus, and formed one of the fleet of Vice-admiral Lord Howe. She continued under Feattus until 1779, when Andrew Sutherland was appointed to command her. In the summer of this year she formed one of the squadron of Sir George Collier that, in conjunction with a land force under Gen. Vaughan, captured Stony Point and Verplanck's Point, on the Hudson. In the month of September of the following year, she conveyed Major Andre up the North River to hold the interview with Arnold, and was the vessel in which that arch traitor made his escape to the British lines. In 1782 she was at Jamaica, and was commanded by Walter Griffith, and in the latter part of the year following she was at Portsmouth. In 1793 she was reported as a hulk, and she appears to have been broken up or otherwise disposed of shortly afterwards.

JAMES FEATTUS was made lieut., 1757, and promoted to commander, July 7, 1761. In 1775 he commanded the sloop Speedwell, and in 1776 was appointed to the Vulture. He died about the year 1785.

(16) JOHN BYRON, second son of William, the fourth Lord Byron by Frances, his third wife, 2d daughter of William Lord

Berkeley, of Stratton, was born Nov. 8, 1723. He served as a midshipman under Commodore Anson on his voyage round the world, and had the misfortune to be cast away in the Wager, on a desolate island, off the coast of Chili, where he suffered great hardships, an affecting account of which will be found in his "Narrative," to which we refer the reader. On the 30th Dec., 1746, he was made post-captain, and appointed to the Syren frigate. In 1753 he commanded the Augusta, of 60 guns, and in 1757 the America, of the same force. In the spring of 1760 he commanded the Fame, of 74 guns, and was employed in the squadron which co-operated with the army at the conquest of Canada, where he rendered important service. In 1764 he made a voyage to the South Sea, and on the 3d June, 1769, was appointed Governor of Newfoundland. In March, 1775, he was made Rear-ad. of the blue, and in May, 1777, Rear of the white. In Jan., 1778, he was made Vice-ad. of the blue, and was soon after appointed to the command of a large squadron, and ordered to North America. He sailed on the 9th of June, and on the 3d of July, a violent gale of wind arose, which dispersed his squadron, Admiral Byron, with his flag on board the Princess Royal, arriving alone off Sandy Hook on the 18th of August. He thence sailed for Halifax, where he found one of his squadron that had arrived before him. The remaining ships came in one by one, with sickly crews and damaged rigging. He was thence ordered to the West Indies, and his action there with D'Estaing, July 6, 1779, though undecisive, was honorable to the British fleet.

Soon after this event he returned to England and struck his flag. He was raised to Vice-ad. of the white, Sept. 6, 1780, and died in London, April 10, 1786, in his 63d year. Though a gallant, zealous and accomplished officer, he was extremely unfortunate, having always the elements to contend with instead of the enemy. Admiral Byron had a family of 2 sons and 7 daughters, by Sarah, daughter of John Trevannion, Esq., of Cartrays, Cornwall, whom he married in 1748. Capt. Byron, one of his sons, was father to the celebrated poet.

(17) The PRINCESS ROYAL was registered as a 2d rate, carried 98 guns, and was built at Portsmouth in 1773. Her length of gun-deck was 177 ft. 6 in., of keel, 145 ft. 5 in., breadth, 50 ft. 6 in., depth in hold, 21 ft., tons, 1,973. In 1777, on the prospect of a rupture with France, Capt. Mark Milbank was appointed to command her; in May Vice-admiral Byron hoisted his flag on board, and on the 5th of June of the following year, she sailed in a strong squadron for America. In 1779 she was commanded by Capt. William Blair, and on the 6th of July was in the action off Grenada with the French fleet, under D'Estaing, when she had 3 of her crew killed and 6 wounded. She returned home soon after. In Dec. she bore the flag of Rear-ad. Hyde Parker, and in the following year composed one of the fleet of Sir George Rodney, in the actions with the French fleet, under Comte de Guichen. In 1781 she was stationed at Jamaica, and she returned home in November. In 1782 she was under the orders of Jonathan Faulkner, and

in Sept. following, sailed in the fleet of Lord Howe to the relief of Gibraltar. In the action with the French and Spanish fleets off Cape Spartel, on the 20th Oct., she had a crew of 750 men, and occupied the 1st or starboard division in the centre squadron in line of battle, which was under the immediate orders of the commander-in-chief. In Jan., 1783, she was at Portsmouth, composing one of the fleet on that station, under Sir Thomas Pye, Admiral of the white. In 1790, on a rupture with Spain being apprehended, Sir William Hotham hoisted his flag on board her as commander of the rear division of the Channel fleet, but the dispute being accommodated, the fleet was dismantled, and Admiral Hotham struck his flag. In 1793 she was one of the squadron of Vice-admiral Cosby; in the following year was under the orders of John Child Purvis, and formed one of the Mediterranean fleet, under Lord Hood. In 1795 Rear-ad. Goodall had his flag on board her, and she bore a part in the engagements with the French, March 14 and July 13th, occupying, in the first engagement, the starboard division in the van squadron, and having a crew of 760 men, of which 3 were killed and 8 wounded. In 1796, being then still under Capt. Purvis, she bore the flag of Vice-ad. Robert Linzee, who was commander of a squadron in the Mediterranean, under Sir John Jervis, Admiral of the blue. In the following year she was under the orders of Capt. John Draper, and was the flag-ship of Sir John Orde, Rear-admiral of the white. In 1799 Capt. J. W. T. Dickson was in command of her, at which time she bore the flag of Rear-ad.

Thomas L. Frederick, and in July she returned home and went into repair. After coming out of dock, Thomas M. Russel was appointed to her, and in 1800 she was one of the fleet of Admiral Lord Bridport, employed on home service. In 1801 she was under the orders of Capt. D. Atkins, and was the flag-ship of Sir Erasmus Gower, who held a command in the Channel fleet; in 1803 she was under Capt. James Vashon, and in the year after was refitting at Chatham. In 1806 she was commanded by Capt. R. C. Reynolds, and she appears to have been broken up or otherwise disposed of about the year 1810.

MARK MILBANK, said by some to have commanded this ship at this time, was the 3d son of Ralph Milbank, Bt., of Halnaby, York Co., and was born about 1721. He was made commander Sept. 13, 1746, and capt., May 21, 1748. He was advanced to Rear-admiral of the white, March 19, 1779, to Vice of the blue, Sept., 26, 1780, and in 1793 became a full admiral. He died on the 10th June, 1805, from a fall over the staircase of his house, in the 84th year of his age.

(b.) SIR RICHARD HUGHES was the son of Sir Richard Hughes, for many years commissioner of the Dock-yard at Portsmouth, and was born in Deptford, Kent Co., Eng., in 1729. When yet a boy, he went to sea as a midshipman, with his father, and in 1741 served in the Mediterranean, under Admiral Matthews. So young was he at this time, that he was under the necessity of shaving his head and wearing a whig to obtain a manly appearance. In 1745 he was made a lieut., and was promoted to the rank of captain, Nov. 10, 1756. He subsequently commanded the Fox and Thames frigates, and in 1768 was appointed to the Firm, of 60 guns, then a guard-ship at Plymouth. After quitting this ship, he was made capt. of the Worcester, of 64 guns, and in 1777 moved into the Centaur, a 74, then employed on the home station. He was afterwards appointed Lieut. Governor of Nova Scotia and commissioner of the Dock-yard at Halifax. This station he filled until his promotion to Rear-ad. of the blue, Sept. 26, 1780, about which time he succeeded, on the death of his father, to the title of baronet. During his stay at Halifax, he caused the woods to be inspected and surveyed, obtained masts, spars and other naval stores for the government dock-yards, on the most advantageous terms, and his conduct otherwise was so meritorious, that on his return home he was honored by the king with a private audience, and received his Majesty's thanks. He became Vice-ad. of the blue in 1790, and on the 14th Feb., 1799, was raised to Admiral of the white. He died on the 5th day of January, 1812. Sir Richard was an active and gallant officer, and in private life possessed all the qualities of a well-bred gentleman. He had a taste for the belles lettres, and possessed also considerable poetical talent. His wife, to whom he was united about 1760, was the grand-niece of the celebrated Sir Hans Sloane, and daughter of Hans Sloane, Esq., M.P., a wealthy and respectable Commoner.

(19) The HAZARD was a British sloop-of-war, mounting 8 guns, and appears to have been built about 1763. In 1767 she was under the orders of Denis Every, and was in the fleet of Vice-admiral Holburne, on home service. In 1769 she was commanded by Thos. Premble, and was at Sheerness, and in 1770 was under the orders of James Orrock, who was succeeded in command of her by John Ford. In 1778 and the year following, she was commanded by Alex. Agnew, in 1780 by G. A. Pulteney, and in the year following by I. Pellew. She appears to have been removed from service soon afterwards.

ALEXANDER AGNEW was made lieut., Aug. 7, 1761, and raised to commander, Nov. 20, 1771. In 1779 he commanded the Hazard sloop, and in 1781 was in command of the sloop Fury of 16 guns. He appears to have died or retired from the service about 1782.

(20) THE French fleet, under M. D'Orvilliers, consisting of 28 sail of the line and several frigates, sailed from Brest, June 4, 1779, for Cadiz, where it formed a junction with the Spanish fleet. The combined fleet, consisting of 66 sail of the line, on the 15th Aug. following, escaping the notice of the English fleet, under Sir Charles Hardy, then cruising in the soundings, sailed up the English Channel, and paraded for three days before Plymouth, insulting the English coast, capturing several coasting vessels, and bidding defiance to the whole

navy. This circumstance greatly tarnished the naval character of England.

(21) The PRINCESS AMELIA was registered as a 3d rate, carried 80 guns, and was built in 1757. In the year following she was commanded by Capt. John Bray, and composed one of the fleet, under Admiral Boscawen, at the reduction of Lewisbourg and Quebec. In Sept., 1759, she was under the orders of Stephen Colby, was the flag-ship of Thomas Broderick, Rear-ad. of the white, and formed one of the fleet of Sir Edward Hawke that was fitted out against Rochfort, and the following year she was under Capt. James Montague, in Admiral Boscawen's fleet in Quiberon Bay. In the spring of 1761 she was in the squadron of Capt. Matthew Buckle, stationed off Brest, to prevent supplies being sent to Belle Isle, and the year after she was under the orders of Capt. Viscount Howe, was the flag-ship of the Duke of York, and composed one of the fleet sent in quest of M. de Ternay, and subsequently one of the fleet of Sir Charles Hardy, that made a cruise in the bay. In 1763 she was under Capt. R. A. Tyrrell, and in 1766 was at Portsmouth. We find her on that station until 1772, when she was commanded by Capt. Samuel Marshall, was the flag-ship of Vice-ad. Geo. B. Rodney, and stationed at Jamaica. In the latter part of the year she returned home, and was laid up at Portsmouth. On the approach of a rupture with France, which took place in 1778, Capt. Digby Dent was appointed to her, and she formed one of the fleet then fitting

for sea at Portsmouth, at which time Sir Thomas Pye had his flag on board. In 1780 she was commanded by Capt. John McCartney, and was one of the fleet of Admiral Geary, then cruising in the Soundings, and the year after, she was the flag-ship of Sir Hyde Parker, and bore a part in the action with the Dutch fleet, under Rear-ad. Zoutman, off the Dogger Bank, Aug. 5. In this engagement, Capt. McCartney and a gunner were killed and three lieuts. wounded. After the death of McCartney, the command of the ship was given to John McBride, and she returned home soon after the battle. In June, 1782, being then under the orders of Billy Douglas, she formed one of the squadron of Lord Howe, cruising in the North Sea, and in July she was cruising with Howe in the Soundings. In October she was commanded by Capt. John Reynolds, was the flag-ship of Sir Richard Hughes, and was one of the fleet of Admiral Lord Howe, that sailed to the relief of Gibraltar, and had a partial action off Cape Spartel with the French and Spanish fleets. On this occasion she was in the 2d or starboard division in the rear squadron, and of a crew of 715 men, had 4 killed and 5 wounded. She was subsequently on duty in the West Indies, under John W. Payne, and the year after returned to England. She came to anchor at Chatham, where she was turned into a church ship. She was used in that capacity until about 1788, shortly after which she was broken up. Her place was supplied by a 74-gun ship of the same name, which in 1800 was building in the king's yard at Chatham.

DIGBY DENT was the son of Capt. Cotton Dent, who died in 1761, one of the captains of Greenwich Hospital. The subject of our notice was made capt., July 7, 1758. In 1778, being then capt. of the Princess Amelia, he received the honor of knighthood at the time the king reviewed the fleet at Portsmouth. On the 24th Sept., 1787, he was advanced to the rank of Rear-admiral, and placed upon the superannuated list. He died, Nov. 15, 1798, leaving his widow and eight children in very distressed circumstances.

(²²) The BRITANNIA was a British ship of the line, registered as a 1st rate, carrying 100 guns, and was built at Portsmouth, Eng., in 1762, to take the place of another ship of the same name and force, which was about that time abandoned. The dimensions of our vessel were as follows: length of gun-deck, 178 feet; keel, 145 feet 2 in.; breadth, 52 ft. ½ in.; depth in hold, 21 ft. 6 in.; tons, 2,091. After being stationed at Portsmouth for several years, in the latter part of 1778, Capt. John Moutray was appointed to her, she being intended as a flag-ship. At the close of the following year, we find her under the command of Capt. Charles Morice Pole, and the flag-ship of George Darby, Vice-ad. of the white, he being at that time the second in command of the Channel fleet, under Sir Charles Hardy. In 1780 she was under the orders of Capt. James Bradby, and was the flag-ship of the fleet, under Vice-ad. Darby, that sailed from Spithead on the 14th day of March, 1781, with a large convoy of victuallers, transports, etc., to the relief of Gibraltar. In December she was the flag-ship of Richard Kempenfelt, Rear-ad. of the white, and was one of his squadron which on the 13th of that month intercepted the French West India convoy that had sailed from Brest under the command of M. de Guichen. In July, 1782, being then under the orders of Capt. Benjamin Hill, she formed one of the fleet of Admiral Lord Howe, cruising in the Soundings, at which time Samuel Barrington, Vice-ad. of the white, had his flag on board her. She subsequently accompanied Lord Howe to intercept the Dutch squadron, and was afterwards at the relief of Gibraltar. In the subsequent encounter which took place with the combined fleets of France and Spain, off Cape Spartel, Oct. 20th, she was in the 1st or starboard division in line of battle, which division was commanded by Vice-ad. Barrington, whose flag-ship she then was. In this engagement, she had 20 of her crew killed and wounded. After this she returned to England, and was put out of commission. On the commencement of the war with France, in 1793, she was again put in service, being then under the orders of Capt. John Holloway, and the flag-ship of Vice-ad. Lord Hotham, who was appointed the second in command of the Mediterranean fleet, under Lord Hood. On the return of the latter to England in Nov., 1794, the command of the squadron became invested in Vice-ad. Hotham, who was employed during the winter in watching the enemy's ports, scouring their coasts, and affording protection to British commerce, and in the month of November, of the following year, she returned home, and was again laid up. In January, 1796, Capt. Shuldham Pearl was appointed to her, and in May following he was succeeded by Capt. Thomas Foley, with Vice-ad. Sir Hyde Parker's flag. In April, 1797, she was the flag-ship of Charles Thomson, Vice-ad. of the blue, and was doing duty in the Mediterranean, being one of the fleet stationed there, under the command of Sir John Jervis, Admiral of the blue. In the month of June, Capt. Edward Marsh was appointed to command her, shortly after which she was fitted up as a hospital-ship, at Portsmouth, and placed under the orders of Lieut. Matthew Connolly. In this capacity we find her in the year 1798 and 1799, and perhaps for several years later. In the year 1803, on the commencement of hostilities, having been thoroughly overhauled, she was placed under the command of Earl Northesk, and proceeded to the Channel, where she served in the fleet stationed there till the following year, when her capt., being promoted Rear-ad. of the white, he soon after hoisted his flag on board her, and continued on the same service till August, 1805, when he was detached with a squadron, under Sir Robert Calder, to reinforce the fleet of Admiral Collingwood, off Cadiz. The Britannia was subsequently in the engagement off Trafalgar, where she was the 4th ship in the lee line in action, and in a short space of time completely dismantled a French ship of 80 guns. She afterwards, singly, engaged and kept at bay three of the enemy's van ships, that were attempting to double upon the Victory, at that time warmly engaged with two of the enemy, and much disabled.

On this occasion the loss of the Britannia was 52 killed and wounded. Soon after the engagement, the Britannia returned to England, and was not again put into commission. She appears to have been broken up about 1813, at which time we find building at Plymouth a 120-gun ship of the same name, the successor to the subject of our notice.

CHARLES MORICE POLE was the 2d son of Reginald Pole, Esq., of Stroke Damarell, and was born Jan. 18, 1757. He was made lieut. in 1773, and obtained post-rank, March 22, 1779. He was made Rear-admiral of the blue, June 1, 1795, Vice-admiral in 1801, and knighted about the same time. In 1805 he was raised to Admiral of the blue, and in 1818 received the Grand Cross of the Bath. He died about the year 1830.

(22) SIR THOMAS PYE was made Capt., April 13, 1741. In 1745 he was one of the members of the court martial convened at Port Mahon for the trial of Capt. Richard Norris. In 1748 he was appointed to the Norwich, in the following year to the Humber, and in the year after was one of the members of the court martial held for the trial of the mutineers on board the Chesterfield. In Feb., 1752, he was appointed to the Advice, of 50 guns, and sent to the West Indies as Commodore on that station. He continued there until 1756, when he was superseded by Commodore Frankland. Charges having been made against him by Mr. Frankland, our officer, in 1758, was brought to a court martial at Portsmouth, when he was reprimanded

for misconduct. In July following he was made Rear-ad. of the blue; in 1759, Rear of the white; in 1760, Rear of the red; and in 1762, was advanced to Vice-ad. of the blue. In 1764 he was appointed Port-admiral at Plymouth, and after serving some time in that position, was again sent to the Leeward Island station, where he remained until 1770, when he returned home. On the 28th of October following, he was made Vice-ad. of the red, and early the succeeding year was sent to the Mediterranean as commander of a small squadron. On his return home he was appointed commander-in-chief at Portsmouth. On the 25th of June, 1773, when the king reviewed the fleet and dockyards at that station, our officer received the honor of knighthood, and was raised to the rank of Admiral of the blue. On the 28th of Jan., 1778, he was advanced to Admiral of the white, and in the same year he acted as President of the court martial held at Portsmouth for the trial of Admiral Keppel. In 1779 he again commanded at Portsmouth, and in 1780 was made Lieut.-general of marines. He died at Marylebone, Feb. 23, 1785. Admiral Pye was one of those men of ordinary capacity, on whom fortune, not merit, often bestows the highest honors. With an awkward figure, and an address by no means pleasing, he was fond of show, and much addicted to intrigue; and to a narrow understanding and shallow attainments, he united an inordinate degree of personal vanity and supercilious consequence. It is painful to see one, who was never signalized by any brilliant achievement, rise by rapid strides to naval rank, and the really brave and worthy tar pine away in anguish and despair, and die unnoticed and forgotten.

(24) The PRINCESS ROYAL Indiaman was captured by the French in the Straits of Sunda, in the year 1793. At the time of her capture, she was under the command of J. Horncastle.

(25) We find the following notices of two of these ships:

"The Ceres, Hawke, and other East India ships, arrived at Crookhaven, in Ireland, in December, 1781."

Gentlemen's Magazine, 1781.

"The Hawke sailed for Bengal on the 16th of November, 1783, and was to be returned from thence to Bombay with a cargo of rice, and then to proceed to China."

Gentlemen's Magazine, 1783.

(26) The English East India Company was incorporated by Queen Elizabeth in 1600, and was empowered to carry on an exclusive trade with "all those new countries to the eastward of the Cape of Good Hope." About the year 1698, application being made to Parliament by private merchants for laying this trade open, an act was passed empowering every subject of England, upon raising a sum for the supply of government, to trade to those parts. Upon this, a great many persons subscribed, and the association thus formed, was called the New East India Company. The old company, being masters of all the forts on the coast of India, the New Company found it

to their interest to unite with them, which they did, and the trade was henceforth carried on with the joint stock, under the style of the United East India Company. The company was formed for purely commercial purposes, and during the first hundred and fifty years of its existence, retained its commercial character, only combining with it so much of warlike enterprise and precaution as was necessary to secure its richly laden ships from being plundered by the fleets of pirates that infested the Indian Seas, and its factories from being burnt or pillaged in the never-ending wars and rebellions among the native chiefs. The company, however, gradually became a corporation of conquerors, and then assumed all the functions of the government of an immense empire, surrendering gradually the operations of traffic to individual merchants, who traded under the shelter of its power. The discipline practiced on board the East India ships was extremely severe. The charter of the company expired within a few years past.

(27) The following articles we take from the newspapers of the day: "LONDON, *August* 5.

* * * * * * *

"As every Rebel, who is taken prisoner has incurred the pain of death by the law martial, it is said that government will charter several transports, after their arrival at Boston, to carry the culprits to the East Indies for the Company's service, as it is the intention of government only to punish the ringleaders and commanders *capitally*, and to suffer the inferior

Rebels to redeem their lives by entering into the East India Company's service. This translation will only render them more useful subjects than in their native country."

* * * * * *

Holts' N. Y. Journal, Thurs., Oct. 19, 1775. *No.* 1711.

"A LETTER FROM BENJAMIN FRANKLIN AND SILAS DEANE, ESQUIRES, TO LORD STORMONT, THE ENGLISH AMBASSADOR AT PARIS.

PARIS, *April* 2, 1777.

My Lord,—

We did ourselves the honor of writing some time since to your Lordship on the subject of exchanging prisoners; you did not condescend to give us any answer, and therefore we expect none to this: we however take the liberty of sending you copies of certain depositions which we shall transmit to Congress, whereby it will be known to your Court, that the United States are not unacquainted with the barbarous treatment their people receive when they have the misfortune of being your prisoners here in Europe; and that if your conduct towards us is not altered, it is not unlikely that severe reprisals may be thought justifiable, from the necessity of putting some check to such abominable practice.

For the sake of humanity it is to be wished that men would endeavour to alleviate as much as possible the unavoidable miseries attending a state of war. It has been said, that among the civilized nations of Europe the ancient horrors of that state are much diminished; but the compelling men by chains, stripes and famine to fight against their friends and relations, is a new mode of barbarity which your nation alone has the honor of inventing, and the sending American prisoners of war to Africa and Asia, remote from all probability of exchange, and where they can scarce hope ever to hear from their families, even if the unwholesomeness of the climate does not put a speedy end to their lives, is a manner of treating captives, that you can justify by no other precedent or custom, except that of the black savages of Guinea.

We are, your Lordship's most obedient humble Servants,

B. FRANKLIN,
S. DEANE.

Lord Viscount
STORMONT."

" To the above letter the following insolent reply was made:

" ' The King's Ambassador receives no Letters from Rebels, except when they come to ask mercy.' "

COPY OF THE DEPOSITIONS ABOVE REFERRED TO.

" The Deposition of Eliphalet Downer, Surgeon, taken in the Yankee privateer, is as follows:

That after he was made prisoner by Captains Ross & Hodge, who took advantage of the generous conduct of Capt. Johnson of the Yankee to them his prisoners, and of the confidence he placed in them in consequence of that conduct and their assurances, he and his countrymen were closely confined, yet assured that on their arrival in port they should be set at liberty, and these assurances were repeated in the most solemn manner, instead of which, on their approach to land they were, in the hot weather of August, shut up in a small cabin, the windows of which were spiked down and no air admitted in, so much that they were all in danger of suffocation from the excessive heat. Three or four days after their arrival in the river Thames, they were relieved from this situation in the middle of the night, hurried on board a tender and sent down to Sheerness, where the deponent was put into the Ardent, and there falling sick of a violent fever in consequence of such treatment, and languishing in that situation for some time, he was removed still sick to the Mars, and notwithstanding repeated petitions to be suffered to be sent to prison on shore, he was detained until having the appearance of a mortification in his legs, he was sent to Haslar hospital, from whence after recovering his health, he had the good fortune to make his escape. While on board those ships and in the hospital, he was informed and believes that many of his countrymen, after experiencing even worse treatment than he, were sent to the East Indies, and many of those taken at Quebec were sent to the coast of Africa as soldiers."

"The Deposition of Captain Seth Clark, of Newbury Port, in the State of Massachusetts-Bay, in America, is as follows:

That on his return from Cape Nichola Mole to Newbury Port, he was taken on the 17th of September last by an armed Schooner in his Britannic Majesty's service, —— Coats, Esq., Commander, and carried down to Jamaica; on his arrival at which place, he was sent on board the Squirrel, another armed vessel, —— Douglass, Esq., Commander, where, although master and half owner of the vessel in which he was taken, he was turned as a common sailor before the mast, and in that situation sailed for England in the month of November, on the 25th of which month they took a schooner from Port a Pe to Charlestown, South Carolina, to which place she belonged, when the owner Mr. Burt, and the master Mr. Bean, were brought on board; on the latter's denying he had any ship papers, Capt. Douglass ordered him to be stripped, tied up and then whipped with a wire cat of nine tails that drew blood every stroke, and then on his saying that he had thrown his papers over board; he was untied and ordered to his duty as a common sailor, with no place for himself or people to lay on but the decks. On their arrival at Spithead, the deponent was removed to the Monarch, and there ordered to do duty as a fore-mast man, and on his refusing on account of inability to do it, he was threatened by the Lieutenant, a Mr. Stoney, that if he spoke one word to the contrary, he should be brought to the gang-way and there severely flogged.

After this he was again removed and put on board the Barfleur, where he remained till the 10th of February. On board this ship the deponent saw several American prisoners, who were closely confined and ironed, with only four men's allowances to six. These prisoners and others informed this deponent that a number of American prisoners had been taken out of the ship and sent to the East Indies and the coast of Africa, which he was told would have been his fate, had he arrived sooner. This deponent further saith, That in Haslar hospital, to which place, on account of sickness, he was removed from the Barfleur, he saw a Captain Chase, of Providence, New England, who told him, that he had been taken in a sloop of which he was half owner and master, on his passage from Providence to South Carolina, by an English transport, and turned over to a ship of war, where he was confined in irons 13 weeks, insulted, beat and abused by the petty officers and common sailors, and on being released from irons was ordered to do duty as a fore-mast man until his arrival in England, when being dangerously ill, he was sent to said hospital.

Paris, March 30, 1777."

Pennsylvania Journal, Aug. 6, 1777.

(₂.) The Jack is the fruit grown on the Jack tree, *Artocarpus jaca*, and is eatable, being of a pleasant flavor. The Jack belongs to the Artocarpeœ family, which are confined entirely to the tropics. The fruit which was eaten by our hero and his companion, and which is also confined to the tropics, was the Manchineal, *Hippomane mancinella*, of the family of Ficarium Cochinchinense, some of the fruit of which is eatable. The Manchineal is very beautiful and attractive in its appearance, and very pleasant when first tasted, but soon becomes so caustic as to corrode the mouth, and occasions severe vomiting, resulting in death. It is exceedingly poisonous, and is often mistaken for the jaca.

(29) We find the following notice of this ship in one of the papers of the day:

"LONDON, Oct. 31.

Capt. Rogers, of the Stormont, East Indiaman, on her passage to St. Helena, took a French snow under American colors, of which he first learned of hostilities being commenced between England and France. Capt. Rogers, thinking himself in danger of being taken, if he continued with his prize, released her, joined the other ships, and acquainted them with the dangerous situation they were in, but fortunately saw no privateers or French men-of-war."

Holt's N. Y. Journal, Mon., March 1, 1779.

(30) The RENOWN was a 4th rate, carried 50 guns, and was built in 1774 as successor to a 40-gun ship which had been broken up. In 1775 our vessel was placed under the orders of Capt. Francis Banks, and ordered to North America, and in the following year she formed one of the fleet of Vice-ad. Lord Howe on that station. In September she was one of the squadron under Sir Peter Parker that co-operated with the army under Sir William Howe, in the reduction of New York. On the 18th day of June, 1777, Capt. Banks died while in command of his vessel, and was succeeded by John Bourmaster. In the following year she was under the orders of George Dawson, and in the month of August, was one of Lord Howe's fleet off Sandy Hook, in the presence of the French fleet. Here she fell in with the Tonnant, of 84 guns, and gave her several broadsides, but other French vessels coming up,

the Renown was obliged to sheer off. Subsequently she engaged the Languedoc, of 90 guns, D'Estaing's own ship, which had lost all her masts, and in that condition was met by Capt. Dawson, who attacked her with resolution, pouring several broadsides into her, carrying away her rudder, and doing her other damage, but the darkness of night prevented him from taking her. On the 5th day of July, 1779, the Renown was one of a squadron, under Sir George Collier, that co-operated with a body of troops, under Major-General Tryon, in the destruction of Fairfield, Norwalk and Greenfield, and in February, 1780, she was one of a squadron that sailed from New York, under Vice-ad. Arbuthnot, to co-operate with Sir Henry Clinton in the reduction of Charleston, South Carolina. In 1781 she was under the command of John Henry, and in December of that year, she formed one of a squadron, under Rear-ad. Kempenfelt, that was sent to intercept the French West India convoy, which had sailed from Brest, under the command of M. de Guichen. In 1782 and the following year she was one of the squadron in North America, under command of Robert Digby, Rear-admiral of the red. She returned to England at the establishment of peace, and in 1784 was undergoing repairs at Chatham. She appears to have been broken up about 1796, in which year we find her successor, a 74-gun ship, building at Dudman's Yard in Deptford.

JOHN HENRY was made lieut., April 27, 1757, promoted to commander, April 16, 1777, and raised to the rank of captain on the 22d day of November following. In 1778 he commanded the 24-gun ship Fowey, and in the month of May of that year, in conjunction with a land force, under Major Maitland, destroyed the American magazines then erecting in the Delaware, and captured the 32-gun frigate Washington and 28-gun frigate Effingham, besides a brig and a sloop. In 1780 he was promoted to the Providence, of 32 guns, an American frigate captured at Charleston, and in the following year was appointed to the Renown, of 50 guns, in which he continued to the end of the war. Capt. Henry died on the 6th day of August, 1829.

(31) The SNARK was a British sloop of 16 guns, and was launched at Hull in 1780. Her predecessor had been purchased by Sir George Rodney, and sailed with him to the West Indies, but foundered on the way. Howell Lloyd, her captain, and part of her crew perished. The sloop which is the subject of our notice was in 1781 under the command of Isaac Vailliant, and in the year following formed one of the squadron in the West Indies, under Commodore Johnston, at which time she was commanded by Robert McDouall. In 1783 she was under the orders of John Maitland, and was cruising in the North Seas, and in the succeeding year she was commanded by Valentine Edwards, and employed on home service. She continued under the latter commander for the usual period, and was then put out of commission. In 1791 she was under the orders of Hon. A. K. Legge, and was

employed as a cruiser in the English and Irish Channels until
1793, when, being under command of Scory Barker, she
formed one of the squadron of Sir Richard King, at Newfoundland. She was subsequently under J. O'Brien, and during the
three following years was attached to the squadron of Sir
James Wallace, who had succeeded King as commander on
that station. After this, she was on duty in the North Sea,
under Francis Warren, and she appears to have been succeeded
in 1799 by another sloop of the same name and force.

ISAAC VAILLIANT was the eldest son of Paul Vailliant, an
eminent bookseller, who held at one time the office of Sheriff
of London. The subject of our note was made lieut., Nov. 25,
1761; commander, Oct. 8, 1777; and capt., Nov. 23, 1780.
In 1777 he commanded the Nabob, an armed vessel, and in
1780 was appointed to the sloop Shark. He was made a
superannuated Rear-admiral in 1799, and died at Blacknell
Banks, Oct. 25, 1804, aged 65 years.

(32) This vessel was lost in November, 1803, near the island
of Fernando de Norhonha, in the South Atlantic Ocean. She
was then used as an artillery transport ship. Her crew and
the artillery troops that had embarked in her, were all taken
off before she sunk. Brig.-Gen. York, of the artillery, was
drowned while endeavoring to reach the shore.

(33) The AMPHITRITE was registered as a sixth-rate, carried
24 guns, and was built in 1778. In the month of May she was

commanded by Thos. Gaborian. In October, 1779, she was under the command of Capt. James Montague, and was cruising off the coast of Spain. In 1780 she was under the orders of Capt. Robert Biggs, and was one of the squadron, under Rear-admiral Thomas Graves, that sailed on the 17th of May for America. In the year following she sailed from Sandy Hook in Admiral Graves' fleet for the Chesapeake. In March, 1782, she took the brig Peggy from Virginia, bound to the West Indies, with a cargo of flour, and in April following she took the privateer ship Franklin. In October, in company with another vessel, she captured two brigs laden with lumber, a ship with silks, from Bilboa, and a privateer schooner, as well as retook two brigs from Virginia, laden with tobacco. She returned to England at the restoration of peace, and went into repair at Woolwich. In 1793 we find her again in commission, she being then under the orders of Capt. Anthony Hunt, 2d, and being one of a squadron of ships that sailed from Spithead for the Mediterranean on the 22d of May, under the command of Vice-ad. Lord Howe. She was wrecked soon after reaching her station, by striking upon a sunken rock. Her captain and crew were all saved. She was succeeded in the navy by a 28-gun frigate that was formerly the Pomona, built at Southampton in 1778 and broken up in 1811.

Robert Biggs was made lieut., Aug. 7, 1761; commander, Jan. 10, 1771; and raised to the rank of captain, March 18, 1778. In 1771 he commanded the Grace, an armed cutter, and in 1774 the sloop Favorite, of 16 guns. In 1778 he commanded the Lively, of 20 guns, and on the 8th day of July of that year, having been ordered to watch the motions of the French fleet off Brest, under Compte D'Orvilliers, upon a fog clearing up, he found himself in the midst of the enemy, whereupon he was compelled to strike his colors. In 1780 he was appointed to the Amphitrite, of 24 guns, and ordered to North America, on which station he remained till the end of the war, when he returned home. He was made Rear-ad. of the white in 1795, Vice-ad. of the blue in 1799, and in the year following was raised to Vice-ad. of the white. He died at Catisfield, Hants, on the 11th day of July, 1803.

(34) The AMPHION was a fifth-rate British frigate, mounting 32 guns, and was launched at Chatham, Dec. 25th, 1780. Her dimensions were as follows: Length of gun-deck, 126 ft. 1 in.; of keel, 104 ft. 3 in.; breadth, 35 ft.; depth, 12 ft. 2 in.; tons, 679. As soon as she was equipped and ready for service, she was placed under the command of Capt. John Bazely; and in the spring of 1781, in company with the Ostridge sloop of war, commanded by Sir Jacob Wheate, and the armed ship Britannia, convoyed to America 23 sail of transports, with about 3,000 German troops, arriving at New York in the month of August, after a passage of 93 days. On the 10th day of September, she formed one of a small squadron, under Capt. Bazely, which in conjunction with a land force, under Gen. Arnold, destroyed the town of New London, with several

magazines of stores, and all the shipping in the harbor. In October following she was one of the fleet, under Rear-ad. Digby, that sailed from New York to the relief of Cornwallis at Yorktown. In the line of battle she was one of the frigates attached to the centre division, which was under the command of Thomas Graves, Rear-ad. of the red. In the month of February, 1782, being on a cruise, in company with the Cyclops frigate, of 28 guns, she captured the Lamblaset, a large French ship, of 16 guns, from Guadaloupe, bound to Virginia, and in the following month she took the French ship La Favourite, of 16 guns, bound from Bayonne in France, to Philadelphia. In May, following, the Amphion made a prize of the schooner Governor Livingston, Captain Moses Griffin, bound from St. Vincent to Philadelphia, and in November she took a sloop, bound from St. Croix to Rhode Island, where she was owned, commanded by Capt. Whipple, and laden with a valuable cargo of rum. The Amphion remained on the American station, under Capt. Bazely, until the end of the war, when she returned home. After being overhauled at Woolwich, Capt. John Brown was appointed to her, and he was succeeded by Capt. Henry Nichols, who in his turn gave up the command to Capt. Herbert Sawyer, under whom, in 1793, she formed one of the fleet of Rear-ad. Kingsmill, on the Irish station. In the following year she appears as one of the squadron at Newfoundland, under Rear-ad. Sir James Wallace. In 1795 Capt. Israel Pellew was appointed to her, under whom she continued a short time at Newfoundland, and returned home the following year. She subsequently cruised a short time in the North Sea, and was then ordered to join the squadron of frigates, under Sir Edward Pellew, employed off the coast of France. On her way thither, having sustained some damage in a hard gust of wind, she put into Plymouth for repair. She anchored in the Sound, Sept. 19, 1796, and went into the harbor the following morning. On the 22d, at about half-past 4 P. M., a violent shock, like that of an earthquake, was felt at Stonehouse, and extended as far off as the Royal Hospital and the town of Plymouth. The sky towards the dock appeared red like the effect of a fire, and for nearly a quarter of an hour the streets were crowded with people running to and fro in the utmost consternation. When the alarm and confusion had somewhat subsided, it was ascertained that the shock had been caused by the explosion of the Amphion. The upper works in the fore part of the ship had been blown to atoms, and she had almost immediately sunk in ten fathoms of water. As the ship was expected to sail the next day, there were nearly 300 persons on board at the time of the calamity. About 100 of these were visitors, who had come to take leave of their friends and relatives before their departure. Of the large number on board, not more than 40 were saved, and the greater portion of these were more or less injured. Capt. Pellew, her commander, was severely wounded, but recovered. Capt. Swaffield, of the Overyssel, who was at dinner with him, was killed, as were also most of the officers who were on board at the time. Several bodies were picked up by the boats. Most of those who remained alive were conveyed in a mangled state to the Royal Hospital. Arms, legs, and lifeless trunks were collected and deposited at the Hospital for identification. As the ship had been originally manned from Plymouth, the number of people who were afterwards seen there in deep mourning for their lost relatives, was truly melancholy. The explosion is supposed to have been caused by the carelessness of the gunner in going among the gunpowder, without using the necessary precautions. The Amphion was succeeded by a frigate of the same name and force, which was built at Betts' yard, in Mistleythorne, in the year 1798.

JOHN BAZELY was born in Dover, in the county of Kent, Eng., about 1740. He entered the navy in 1755, and became lieut., April 7, 1760. On the 22d Sept., 1777, while in command of the Alert cutter, of 10 guns and 60 men, he captured the brig Lexington, of 16 guns and 84 men, of whom 7 were killed and 11 wounded. The Alert had 2 killed and 3 wounded. For this achievement he was promoted to the rank of commander. On the 15th April, 1778, he was advanced to post-captain in the Formidable, of 90 guns, the flag-ship of Sir Hugh Palliser, in the fleet under the command of Admiral Keppel. In the action off Brest on the 27th July, he was, of course, present, and his ship had a greater number of killed and wounded than any other of the fleet. Capt. Bazely was subsequently moved to the Pegasus, of 28 guns. On the 8th

Jan., 1780, he participated in the capture of a valuable Spanish convoy, and on the 16th of the same month was engaged in the action with the Spanish fleet off Cadiz. He afterwards, for a short time, commanded the frigate Apollo, and was then appointed to the Amphion, of 32 guns, in which he continued to the end of the American war. On the return of peace he was appointed to the Alfred, of 74 guns, then a guard-ship at Chatham, and was subsequently under Howe in the memorable engagement of 1st June, 1794. He afterwards moved to the Blenheim, of 98 guns, and served in her, under Admiral, Lord Hotham, in the Mediterranean. On the 1st June, 1795, he was made Rear-ad. of the white, and by subsequent promotions attained the rank of Vice-ad. of the red. He died at Dover, April 6, 1809, at the age of 69 years.

(26) The "JERSEY" was originally a British ship of the line. She was registered as a 4th-rate, carried 60 guns, and was built in 1736, as successor to a 50-gun ship, which had been condemned as unfit for further duty. The first service of our ship was in 1737, when she was one of the Channel fleet, under Sir John Norris. In 1739 she was commanded by Edmund Williams, and composed one of the Mediterranean fleet, under Rear-admirals Nicholas Haddock and Sir Chaloner Ogle, and she was subsequently one of the squadron that was designed against Ferrol. In 1741 she was commanded by Peter Lawrence, and in March of that year, she bore the flag of Sir Chaloner Ogle, at which time she composed one of the fleet of

Admiral Vernon, in his unsuccessful expedition against Carthagena. In 1743 Harry Norris was appointed to her, who in 1744 was succeeded in command of her by Charles Hardy, subsequently Governor of New York. Under this officer she formed, in the following year, one of the Mediterranean fleet, under Vice-admiral Rowley. On the 26th of July, while on a cruise off Gibraltar, she fell in with the St. Esprit, a French ship of 74 guns. An engagement ensued, and lasted for $2\frac{1}{2}$ hours, when the St. Esprit, being much damaged, was compelled to sheer off. The Jersey being also much crippled, was unable to pursue her, and accordingly put into Lisbon for repair. She subsequently served in the Mediterranean fleet, under Admiral Medley, and then returned home. In Oct., 1748, the Jersey was reported as a hulk, and in 1755, after being put into repair at Chatham, and manned with a crew of 420 men, she was placed under the orders of Sir William Burnaby, in anticipation of a rupture with France. In 1757 John Barker was appointed to her, and under him she formed one of the Mediterranean fleet, under Henry Osborne, Admiral of the blue. In 1759 she composed one of the fleet of Admiral Boscawen, in his maneuvers against the French squadron, under M. de la Clue, and she was one of the three ships that made the unsuccessful attempt to cut away two of the enemy's vessels in the harbor of Toulon. About the latter part of the year Andrew Wilkinson was appointed to her, under whom she composed one of the Mediterranean fleet, under Vice-admiral Saunders, until near the termination of the war. In

1766 William Dickson was appointed to command her as captain to Sir Richard Spry, who hoisted his flag on board, and continued in her as commander of a small squadron in the Mediterranean till 1768. In the following year she sailed from Plymouth for Newfoundland, taking the Hon. John Byron, the newly appointed Governor of that colony, as a passenger, and bearing his flag on board. She returned home at the end of the year and put into Chatham, where she was soon after fitted up as a hospital-ship. She was placed under the orders of Commander W. A. Halstead, and sailed for America in the spring of 1776, as one of the squadron of Commodore Hotham, arriving at Sandy Hook in the month of August. She subsequently was used for a short time as a store-ship, then employed again as a hospital-ship, and finally fitted up as a prison-ship, in which capacity she remained till the termination of the war, when she was broken up and sunk off the Long Island shore, near the site of the present navy yard. She was succeeded in the navy by a cutter of the same name, which was launched in 1860.

For further particulars respecting her, the sufferings of the prisoners on board, etc., see "Adventures of Christopher Hawkins," etc., edited by Charles I. Bushnell. 8vo. pp. 316. N. Y., 1864. See also Appendix to the present volume.

(₃₆) Capt. BENJAMIN ELLINGWOOD was the great-grandson of Ralph Ellingwood, one of the first settlers of Beverly, Mass., and was the son of Ebenezer Ellingwood. His mother's maiden name was Elizabeth Corning. The subject of our sketch was born in Beverly, Aug. 16, 1753, and died in the West Indies in the summer of 1792. The following is his genealogy, taken from the Town Records:

RALPH ELLINGWOOD, married Aug. 21, 1691. Had one son, viz.:
EBENEZER ELLINGWOOD, born Aug. 29, 1697. Married Sarah Tuck, March 23, 1719. Had one son, viz.:
EBENEZER ELLINGWOOD, born Oct. 30, 1719. Married Elizabeth Corning, May 24, 1744. Had one son, viz.:
BENJAMIN ELLINGWOOD, born Aug. 16, 1753. Married Ann Clark, Nov. 17, 1774. No children. He married Love Hilton, Aug. 8, 1779. No descendants living.

(35) CAPE ANN, a promontory in Essex Co., Mass. It derives its name from Prince Charles, who gave it the name out of respect to his mother, Queen Ann, the consort of James 1st. Sandy Bay, now called Rockport, is on the north-easterly side of the Cape, about four miles from the South Harbor.

(36) JOHN BLATCHFORD, Senr., the father of our hero, was born in the southern part of England, about the year 1702. In 1716, when the river Thames was frozen over, and when beeves were roasted and eaten on the ice, he was present with hundreds of men and boys. "After the gentlemen had finished their feast," as he himself used to say, "the boys were all bountifully supplied." At this time he called himself 14 years old. Some years after this remarkably cold winter, Mr. Blatchford came to Portsmouth, N. H., where he resided

several years, and then moved to Salem, Mass. He came to Gloucester, now Rockport, on Cape Ann, about 1754. Here, Jan. 7, 1755, he married Rachel, daughter of Samuel and Elizabeth Clark, of that place. For many years preceding his death, Mr. Blatchford was very infirm, and his wife being unable to take care of him, they went to live with their daughter Rachel. There Mrs. Blatchford died in the year 1800. Mr. Blatchford continued residing with his daughter until 1809, when he died at the age of about 107 years. The following were the names of his children :

1. MOLLY...... Married 1st. Mr. Craven. 2d. Joseph Tucker.
2. JOHN........ " Anna, d. of Nehemiah and Betsey Grover.
3. WILLIAM....   Died young.
4. RACHEL..... " Nathaniel Foster, of Woolwich, Me.
5. SAMUEL..... " Lydia, d. of Henry Clark, of Rockport.
6. NATHANIEL.. " Abigail Cleveland, of Gloucester.
7. HENRY...... " Hannah, d. of John and Anna Gamage, of Rockport.
8. JONATHAN...   Died young.

(39) We have stated that the maiden name of Mr. Blatchford's wife was Anna Grover. This lady was born in 1766, and was the daughter of Nehemiah Grover, a farmer of Sandy Bay, now Rockport. Her mother, Betsey Grover, was the daughter of Nathaniel Gamage, by his wife Mary, daughter of Joshua Norwood.

Mr. Blatchford died about the year 1794, leaving his widow surviving him. In the year 1800 she married Edward Higgins, Jr., and he dying in 1805, she was again left a widow.

She supported herself and children by weaving, until the factories so affected the wheel and loom, that that trade became no longer remunerative. She then devoted a part of her time to nursing the sick, in which occupation she was held in great repute. She is represented as having been of an amiable disposition, of industrious habits, and possessed of many endearing qualities. She died on the fourth day of March, 1841, at the age of 75 years.

Her children by Mr. Blatchford were as follows:

NANCY....born 1784.....................................Died young.
RACHEL... " 1786....married Francis Hilton, of Gloucester........
                                                She is still living.
WILLIAM.. " 1788.... " 1st. Betsey Foster. 2d. Mrs. Mary Tarr, of Rockport. He died, Jan. 20, 1864.
JOHN..... " 1790.... " Margaret Oakes Soper, of Rockport.
                                                He is still living.

For the following additional particulars, we are indebted to the kindness of Miss Betsie F. Andrews, of Rockport, Mass.

RACHEL BLATCHFORD, eldest child of John Blatchford and Anna (Grover) Blatchford, that arrived at maturity, was born in Rockport in 1786. Married Francis Hilton, of Gloucester, who died at Rockport, 1812. Mrs. Hilton has since remained a widow, and is at this date (1865) living with her daughter, Sarah, in Cambridge, Mass. Her children are as follows:

1. FRANCIS....born 1806..married, 1st, Mary Pew. 2d, Sarah Tappan.
                                                Still living in Gloucester.

2. SARAH.....born 1803..married, 1st, David Mellen. 2d, James Hilton.
Still living in Cambridge.
3. WILLIAM... " 1810..unmarried.............Died.
4. ISAAC TULL. " 1810..married, 1st, Rhoda Poole. He died and his
widow married Chas. Marchant, who died.

WILLIAM BLATCHFORD, brother of the preceding, was born in Rockport, 1788; married (1814), 1st, Betsey Foster, daughter of Nathaniel and Rachel Foster, of Rockport, who died, Jan., 1831. 2d, (1833) Mary Tarr, widow of Robert Tarr, and daughter of George and Sally Gott, all of Rockport. William Blatchford was a resident of Rockport, and was a very enterprising seaman. In 1799, when only 11 years of age, he served on board the "Congress." When past 70 years old, he received a land warrant for that service. He died, Jan. 20, 1864. His children were—

By his first marriage.

1. CAROLINE PREBLE..born June 20, 1815..........Died young.
2. WILLIAM.......... " July 17, 1817..married Ellen Reid, of Paterson, N. J.
3. MARY POLLARD.... " Feb. 22, 1819.. " Charles Nute, of Dover, N. H.
4. JOHN............. " Aug. 13, 1821.. " Lydia White, of Casco, Me.
5.   A Daughter.... " July 15, 1823.. Died an infant.
6. NANCY G.......... " Sept. 5, 1825.. " John Pittee.
7. ELIZABETH........ " Sept. 8, 1827.. " Daniel Merrill, of Buxton, Me.
8. DUDLEY CHOATE... " Dec. 12, 1829.. " Mary Ann Babson, of Rockport.
9. NATHANIEL FOSTER. " Nov. 29, 1831.. " Mary Findlay.

By his second marriage.

1. BENJAMIN FRANKLIN..born Jan.   1835..married Emily Snow. He served in the War for the Union in 2d Mass. Artillery, and was promoted 1st lieut. for gallant conduct.
2. LUCY SANBORN....... " Sept. 8, 1838..........Died young.
3. LOUISA FOSTER....... " Nov. 29, 1841...married Henry Martin Lowe, of Rockport, who served in the War for the Union.

Capt. JOHN BLATCHFORD, brother of the preceding, and the youngest of the children of John Blatchford, and Anna his wife, was born in Rockport, 1790; married, 1809, Margaret Oakes, daughter of Benjamin Soper. Mr. and Mrs. Blatchford are still living in Rockport, in the State of Massachusetts. Their children are as follows:

1. CHARLOTTE FOSTER....born Dec. 1, 1809..married, 1st, Lemuel Norwood, keeper of the "Light" on Eastern Point, Gloucester. 2d, Daniel Norwood, of Gloucester.
2. MARGARET OAKES......born Dec. 16, 1811..married William Thurston, of Rockport.
3. JOHN................. " Oct. 15, 1812........Died young.
4. SALLY FOSTER......... " Apl. 21, 1814..married John Hoble, of Rockport.
5. CAROLINE PREBLE...... " Apl. 28, 1817..married Benjamin Soper Marshall, Jr., of Rockport.
6. MARY CHOATE......... " Feb. 4, 1821..married Albert Giddings Hale.
7. SOPHIA ANDREWS...... " Oct. 5, 1823........Died young.

8. NANCY TARR. ....born July 26, 1826..married James Munroe Montgomery, of Boothbay, Me.
9. JOHN................. " Oct. 15, 1827........Died young.
10. ZELINDA GOSS......... " Aug. 26, 1828..married Benjamin Reed Montgomery, of Boothbay, Me.
11. LOUISA MARIA MELLEN. " Dec. 11, 1833..married David Parsons Boynton, Jr., of Rockport, who served in Co. B, 50th Regt. Mass. Vols., in War for the Union, and died in Rockport, Nov. 3, 1863.
12. BETSEY FOSTER........ " Mar. 11, 1836..married John Edmunds, of Rockport.

APPENDIX.

The DESTRUCTIVE OPERATION *of* FOUL AIR, TAINTED PROVISIONS, BAD WATER, *and* PERSONAL FILTHINESS, *upon* HUMAN CONSTITUTIONS; *exemplified in the unparalleled Cruelty of the British to the American Captives at New-York during the Revolutionary War, on Board their Prison and Hospital Ships. By Captain* ALEXANDER COFFIN, *Jun., one of the surviving Sufferers: In a Communication to Dr.* MITCHILL, *dated September 4,* 1807.

I SHALL furnish you with an account of the treatment that I, with other of my fellow citizens received on board the *Jersey* and *John* prison ships; those monuments of British barbarity and infamy. I shall give you nothing but a plain simple statement of facts that cannot be controverted. And I begin my narrative from the time of my leaving the South-Carolina frigate.

In June, 1782, I left the above mentioned frigate in the Havanna, on board of which ship I had long served as a midshipman, and made several trading voyages. I sailed early in September from Baltimore for the Havanna, in a fleet of about forty sail, most of which were captured, and we among the rest, by the British frigate Ceres, Captain Hawkins, a man in every sense of the word a perfect brute. Although our commander, Captain Hughes, was a very gentlemanly man, he was treated in the most shameful and abusive manner by said Hawkins, and ordered below to mess with the petty officers. Our officers were put in the cable-tier with the crew, and a guard placed at the hatchway to prevent more than two going on deck at a time, and that only for the necessary calls of nature. The provisions served out to us were of the very worst kind, and very short allowance even of that. They frequently gave us pea-soup, that is, pea-water, for the pease and the soup, all but about a gallon or two, were taken out for the ship's company, and the coppers filled up with water, and just warmed and stirred together, and brought down to us in a strap-tub. And, Sir, I might have defied any person on earth, possessing the most acute olfactory powers, and the most refined taste, to decide, either by one or the other, or both of those senses, whether it was pease and water, slush and water, or swill. After living and being treated in this way, subject to every insult and abuse for ten or twelve days, we fell in with the Champion British twenty-gun ship, which was bound to New York to refit, and were all sent on board of her. The Captain was a true seaman and a gentleman; and our treatment was so different from what we had experienced on board the Ceres, that it was like being removed from purgatory to paradise. His name, I think, was Edwards. We arrived about the beginning of October at New-York, and were immediately sent on board the prison-ship in a small schooner called, ironically enough, the *Relief*, commanded by one Gardner, an Irishman. This schooner *Relief* plied between the prison-ship and New-York, and carried the water and provisions from the city to the ship. In fact, the said schooner might emphatically be termed the *Relief*, for the execrable water and provisions she carried *relieved* many of my brave but unfortunate countrymen *by death*, from the misery and savage treatment they daily endured. Before I go on to relate the treatment we experienced on board the *Jersey*, I will make one remark, and that is, that if you were to rake the infernal regions, I doubt whether you could find such another set of dæmons as the officers and men who had charge of the old *Jersey* prison-ship. And, Sir, I shall not be surprised if you, possessing those finer feelings which I believe are interwoven in the composition of man, and which are not totally torn from the *piece*, till, by a long and obstinate perseverance in the meanest, the basest, and cruelest of all human arts, a man becomes lost to every sense of honour, of justice, of humanity, and common honesty;—I shall not be surprised, I say, if you, possessing those finer feelings, should doubt whether men could be so lost to their sacred obligations to their God, and the moral ties which ought to bind them to their duty toward their fellow men, as those men were, who had the charge, and also those who had any agency in the affairs of the *Jersey* prison-ship. *On my arrival on board the old Jersey, I found there about eleven hundred prisoners; many of them had been there from three to six months, but few* lived over that time if they did not get away by some means or other. They were generally in the most deplorable situation, mere walking skeletons, without money, and scarcely clothes to cover their nakedness, and overrun with lice from head to foot. The provisions, Sir, that were served out to us was not more than four or five ounces of meat, and about as much bread, all condemned provisions from their ships of war, which no doubt were supplied with new in their stead, and the new in all probability charged by the commissaries to the Jersey. They, however, know best about that; and however secure they may now feel, they will have to render an account of that business to a Judge who cannot be deceived. This fact, however, I can safely aver, that both the times that I was confined on board the prison-ship, there never were provisions served out to the prisoners that would have been eatable by men that were not literally in a starving situation. The water that we were forced to use was carried from this city; and I positively assert, that I never, after having followed the sea thirty years, had on board of any ship, (and I have been three years on some of my voyages) water so bad as that we were obliged to use on board the old Jersey; when there was, as it were to tantalize us, as fine water, not more than three cables length from us, at the mill in the Wallabout, as was perhaps ever drank.

There were hogs kept in pens on the gun-deck by the officers of the prison-ship for their own use; and I have seen the prisoners watch an opportunity, and with a tin pot steal the bran from the hogs' trough, and go into the galley, and when *they could get an opportunity, boil it on the fire, and eat it as you, Sir, would eat of good soup when hungry.* This I have seen more than once, and there are those now living beside me who can bear testimony to the same fact. There are many other facts equally abominable that I could mention, but the very thought of those things brings to my recollection scenes the most distressing. When I reflect how many hundreds of my brave and intrepid brother-seamen and countrymen I have seen in all the bloom of health, brought on board of that ship, and in a few days numbered with the dead, in consequence of the savage treatment they there received; I can but adore my Creator that he suffered me to escape; but I did not escape, Sir, without being brought to the very verge of the grave. This was the second time I was on board, which I shall mention more particularly hereafter. Those of us who had money fared much better than those who had none. I had made out to save, when taken, about twenty dollars, and with that I could buy from the bumboats that were permitted to come along side, bread, fruit, &c., but, Sir, those bumboatmen were of the same kidney with the officers of the *Jersey;* we got nothing from them without paying through the nose for it, and I soon found the bottom of my purse; after which I fared no better than the rest. I was, however, fortunate in another respect; for after having been there about six weeks, two of my countrymen, (I am a Nantucket man) happened to come to New-York to endeavour to recover a whaling sloop that had been captured, with a whaling licence from Admiral Digby;

and they found means to procure my release, passing me for a Quaker, to which I confess I had no pretensions further than my mother being a member of that respectable society. Thus, Sir, I returned to my friends fit for the newest fashion, after an absence of three years. For my whole wardrobe I carried on my back, which consisted of a jacket, shirt, and trousers, a pair of old shoes, and a handkerchief served me for a hat, and had more than two months, for I lost my hat the day we were taken, from the main-top-gallant-yard, furling the top-gallant-sail. My clothes, I forgot to mention, were completely laced with locomotive tinsel, and moved, as if by instinct, in all directions; but as my mother was not fond of such company, she furnished me with a suit of my father's, who was absent at sea, and condemned my laced suit for the benefit of all concerned.

Being then in the prime of youth, about eighteen years of age, and naturally of a roving disposition, I could not bear the idea of being idle at home. I therefore proceeded to Providence, Rhode Island, and shipping on board the brig Betsey and Polly, Captain Robert Folger, bound for Virginia and Amsterdam, we sailed from Newport early in February, 1783; and were taken five days after off the capes of Virginia, by the Fair American privateer, of this port, mounting sixteen sixes, and having eighty-five men, commanded by one Burton, a refugee, most of whose officers were of the same stamp. We were immediately handcuffed two and two, and ordered into the hold in the cable-tier. Having been plundered of our beds and bedding, the softest bed we had was the soft side of a water cask and the coils of a cable. The Fair American having been handsomely dressed by an United States vessel of one half of her force, was obliged to put into New-York, then in possession of the British enemy, to refit; and we arrived within the Hook about the beginning of March, and were put on board a pilot boat and brought up to this city. The boat hauled along side of the Crane-wharf, where we had our irons knocked off, *the marks of which I carry to this day;* and were put on board the same schooner *Relief* mentioned in a former part of this narrative, and sent up once more to the prison-ship. It was just three months from my leaving the *old Jersey*, to my being again a prisoner on board of her; and on my return I found but very few of those whom I had left three months before; some had made their escape; some had been exchanged; *but the greater part had taken up their abode under the surface of that hill which you can see from your windows, where their bones are mouldering to dust, and mingling with mother earth; a lesson to Americans, written* IN CAPITALS, ON BRITISH CRUELTY AND INJUSTICE. *I found, on my return on board the Jersey, more prisoners than when I left her; and she being so crowded, they were obliged to send about two hundred of us on board the John, a transport ship of about three hundred tons.* There we were treated worse, if possible, than on board the Jersey; and our accommodations were infi-nitely worse, for the Jersey being an old condemned sixty-four gun ship, had two tier of ports fore and aft, air ports and large hatchways, which gave a pretty free circulation of air through the ship; whereas the John being a merchant ship, and with small hatchways, and no ports, and the hatches laid down every night, and no man allowed during the night to go on deck, all exonerations were of course made below; the effluvia arising from these, together with the already contaminated air occasioned by the breath of so many people so pent up together, was enough to destroy men of the most healthy and robust constitutions. All the time I was on board this ship not a prisoner eat his allowance, bad as it was, cooked, more than three or four times; but eat it raw as it came out of the barrel. These, Sir, are stubborn facts that cannot be controverted. In the middle of this ship, between decks, was raised a platform of boards about two and a half feet high, for those prisoners to sleep on who had no hammocks. On this they used frequently to sit and play at cards to pass the time. One night in particular, several of us sat to see them play till about ten o'clock, and then retired to our hammocks, and left them playing; about one A. M. we were called and told that one *Bird* was dying; we turned out and went to where he lay, and found him just expiring. Thus, at ten P. M. this young man was apparently as well as any of us, and at one A. M. had paid the debt to nature. Many others went off in the same way. It will perhaps be said that men may die suddenly any where. True; but do they die suddenly any where from the same cause? After all these things, it is, I think, impossible for the mind to form any other conclusion than that there was a premeditated design to destroy as many Americans as they could on board of their prison-ships; the treatment of the prisoners warrants the conclusion; but it is mean, base and cowardly, to endeavour to conquer an enemy by such infamous means, and truly characteristic of base and cowardly wretches. The truly brave will always treat their prisoners well. There were two or three hospital ships near the prison ships; and so soon as any of the prisoners complained of being sick, they were sent on board of one of them; and I verily believe that not one out of a hundred ever returned or recovered. I am sure I never knew but one to recover. Almost (and in fact I believe I may safely say) *every morning a large boat from each of the hospital ships went loaded with dead bodies, which were all tumbled together into a hole dug for the purpose, on the hill where the national navy-yard now is.* A singular affair happened on board of one of those hospital-ships, and no less true than singular. All the prisoners that died after the boat with the load had gone ashore, were sewed up in hammocks, and left on deck till the next morning. As usual, a great number had thus been disposed of. In the morning, while employed in loading the boat, one of the seamen perceived motion in one of the hammocks, just as they were about launching it down the board placed for that purpose from the gunwale of the ship into the boat, and exclaimed, D——n my eyes, that fellow is not dead; and, if I have been rightly informed, and I believe I have, there was quite a dispute between this man and the others about it. They swore he was dead enough, and should go into the boat; he swore he should not be launched, as they termed it, and took his knife and ripped open the hammock, and behold! the man was really alive. There had been a heavy rain during the night, and as the vital functions had not totally ceased, but were merely suspended in consequence of the main spring being out of order, this seasonable moistening must have given tone and elasticity to the great spring, which must have communicated to the lesser ones, and put the whole machinery again in motion. You know better about these things than I do, and can better judge of the cause of the re-animation of this man from the circumstances mentioned. He was a native of Rhode-Island; his name was Gavot. He went to Rhode-Island in the same flag of truce with me about a month afterwards. I felt extremely ill, but made out to keep about till I got home (my parents then lived on the island of Nantucket); was then taken down, and lay in my bed six weeks in the most deplorable situation; my body was swelled to a great degree, and my legs were as big round as my body now is, and affected with the most excruciating pains. What my disorder was I will not pretend to say; but Dr. Tupper, quite an eminent physician, and a noted tory, who attended me, declared to my mother that he knew of nothing that would operate in the manner that my disorder did but poison. For the truth of this I refer to my father and brothers, and to Mr. Henry Coffin, father to Captain Peter Coffin, of the Manchester Packet of this port.

Thus, Sir, in some haste, without much attention to order

or diction, I have given you part of the history of my life and sufferings; but I endeavoured to bear them as became an American. And I must mention, before I close, to the everlasting honour of those unfortunate Americans who were on board the Jersey prison-ship, that notwithstanding the savage treatment they received, and death staring them in the face, every attempt (which was very frequent) that the British made to persuade them to enter on board their ships of war or in their army, was treated with the utmost contempt; and I never knew, while I was on board, but one instance of defection, and that person was hooted at and abused by the prisoners till the boat was out of hearing. The patriotism in preferring such treatment, and even death in its most frightful shapes, to the serving the British, and fighting against their own country, has seldom been equalled, certainly never excelled. And if there be no monument raised with hands to commemorate the virtue of those men, it is stamped in capitals on the heart of every American acquainted with their merit and sufferings, and will there remain so long as the blood flows from its fountain.

Medical Repository, Vol. xi., or Vol. v. of 2d Hexade, pp. 260-267.

www.ingramcontent.com/pod-product-compliance
Lightning Source LLC
Chambersburg PA
CBHW031600170426
43196CB00032B/713